Marxism and Historical Writing

Paul Q. Hirst

Routledge & Kegan Paul

LONDON AND NEW YORK

First published in 1985
Reprinted and first published as a paperback in 1986
by Routledge & Kegan Paul Ltd.,

11 New Fetter Lane, London EC4P 4EE

Published in the USA by
Routledge & Kegan Paul Ltd.
in association with Methuen Inc.
29 West 35th Street, New York NY10001

Set in 10 on 12 point Sabon
by Set Fair
and printed in Great Britain
by Thetford Press Limited,
Thetford, Norfolk

Library of Congress Cataloging in Publication Data

Hirst, Paul Q.

Marxism and historical writing.
Bibliography: p.
1. Historiography—Addresses, essays, lectures.
2. Historical materialism—Addresses, essays, lectures.
I. Title.
D13.2.H47   1985   907.2   84-9969

British Library CIP data also available.

ISBN 0-7102-1105-8

Contents

Preface

The theory of history remains a perennial field of debate within Marxism. Not surprisingly since most Marxists have considered the centrepiece of Marx's achievement to be 'historical materialism', a science of history. In *Pre-Capitalist Modes of Production* Barry Hindess and I challenged this judgment. We argued that the theory of modes of production could not progress if it was viewed as part of a philosophy of history and we also questioned the all too easy assimilation that had taken place in Britain between Marxism and the historian's practice. Our work produced an expected reaction of disbelief and rejection on the part of many Marxists, especially those who were professional historians. It also produced another set of reactions. On the one hand, a grudging acceptance by some Marxists that we were not without powerful arguments for our case. On the other hand, an enthusiastic acceptance by some Marxist philosophers and theorists who saw the need for a radical re-thinking of the role of Marxist theory if it was to serve as a guide to contemporary political practice in the advanced capitalist West. This book is an attempt to bring the debate up to date since our original contribution in 1975.

It reproduces two essays which address the work of two of the leading Marxist historians in Great Britain, Perry Anderson and E. P. Thompson. The first (Chapter 4) is a critical rebuttal of E. P. Thompson's *The Poverty of Theory*, which was first published in 1979, shortly after Thompson's own book. Thompson attempted to stave off the mushrooming popularity of Louis Althusser and the growing influence of our own work in a critique of unprecedented violence and abusiveness. The second (Chapter 5) is a critical appraisal of Anderson's work on the absolutist state and an attempt to show how and why it fails to address the problems about the theory of modes of production we outlined in *Pre-Capitalist Modes of Production*, published at about the same time as Anderson's own books. These essays remain relevant today and I have re-published them at the suggestion of friendly readers who have encouraged me to put them before the public in a more accessible form.

At the same time more needs to be said. In the first chapter in this volume I have attempted to bring the debate up to date. Reviewing in particular Anderson's attempt to settle accounts with Thompson in *Arguments within English Marxism*, Anderson's and Thompson's enterprises are re-considered, and their respective strengths and weaknesses re-assessed. My own general position on Marxism and historical writing is re-stated and revised. In particular, I have tried to show how Anderson's own position, for all its attempt to do justice to both Thompson and Althusser, fails to address some of their most positive endeavours, and also how he has failed to address or answer the points made by myself and my co-authors. This first chapter serves as a general introduction to the volume.

G. A. Cohen's book on Marx has received lavish praise as a defence of the traditional account of 'historical materialism'. Anderson is one of the leading voices in this chorus. In the second chapter I have tried to show that Cohen's 'defence' is neither faithful to Marx nor does it succeed in its own terms.

The third chapter in the book is a sympathetic exposition of R. G. Collingwood's theory of the historian's practice. I make no pretence that it is my own. On the other hand, I believe that Marxists should read and learn from Collingwood's work. He is a neglected figure of major stature. Marxists will by and large not agree with what Collingwood says. I hope that they will see both that he explodes the myth of historical 'evidence', epitomised in E. P. Thompson's claim that the given 'facts' of history constitute a court in which theories of history are tried. I also hope they will see how Collingwood's insistence on history being written from the stand-point of the present is in some ways a better account of Thompson's practice than his own and that it defends the notion of a 'strategic' historiography informed by current concerns rather than an endless poking in the potentially infinite archive of the 'past'. History without this strategic dimension can be a diversion for the Left.

The essays on Anderson and Thompson, and the first chapter, 'Anderson's Balance Sheet', make clear the ways in which historical writing is informed by the historian's point of view of politics and the tasks which face us in politics. For this reason I have included two chapters which make my own political concerns clear. Chapter 7, 'Labour's Crisis', outlines my own conceptions of contemporary politics and Chapter 8, 'Obstacles in the Parliamentary Road' – a sympathetic account of aspects of Nicos Poulantzas's *State, Power, Socialism* – is an attempt to make clear my own view of the relationship between parliamentary electoral politics and democratic socialism. The chapter on Poulantzas first appeared in a little-known journal called *Euro-Red*. I have also included an interview in the course of which I review my general theoretical and political position. The interview was published in an Australian journal called *Local Consumption*, and was conducted by Peter Botsman, Judith Allen and Paul Patton.

In this collection I have tried to settle accounts justly and honestly with Louis Althusser and Nicos Poulantzas, both of whom have been tragically silenced, the former by mental illness and the murder of the person closest to him, and the latter by suicide. I cannot hide my sorrow and distress at these events. At the same time one must insist that their personal tragedies do not invalidate their respective intellectual and political enterprises. Justice and honesty consist in taking what they did seriously and making clear what is valuable in that work, but also where one differs.

This book does not pretend to be an exhaustive review on the subject of Marxism and historiography. It will doubtless not be my final view on the subject. It is ruthlessly selective but in the manner of Lenin's injunction that while it is permissible in military affairs to attack weakness, victory is victory whatever the point one chooses to strike at the enemy's line, in matters of theory one must attack positions of strength, frontally and openly. I would claim that Anderson, Cohen and Thompson each offer in their own ways strong positions, positions with flaws which admit of criticism and rebuttal but which must be addressed. I expect no more and no less in return. We cannot fear active critical debate. What we must avoid, both as socialists concerned to behave in a comradely spirit, and as intellectuals concerned to preserve the possibility of reasoned debate, is *ad hominem* abuse and the obfuscation of one's

grounds for difference. I leave it to the reader to judge the measure
of my own success.

I have to thank the editors of *Economy and Society* and *Local
Consumption* for their kind permission to reproduce Chapters 4
and 5, and 6 respectively. I am also particularly indebted to the
efforts of Roland Anrup, Mark Cousins, Michael Cowen, Stephen
Feuchtwang, Barry Hindess and Maxine Molyneaux in reading the
manuscript and offering prompt and invaluable critical comments.
Many such acknowledgments are ritual *politesse*, in this case they
are probably far less than their recipients deserve.

Chapter 1

Anderson's Balance Sheet

Perry Anderson's *Arguments within English Marxism* is a remarkable achievement, for in this book he manages a balanced and sympathetic critical assessment of his old adversary Edward Thompson. To one who recalls the furious debate occasioned by the publication of 'The Origins of the Present Crisis' in 1964–6 as a vital part of his intellectual formation, Anderson's generosity of spirit is surprising and admirable. For if ever there was an intellectual 'police action', Thompson's essay 'The Peculiarities of the English' (in *The Poverty of Theory*) must be it. This riposte was intended as a crushing, silencing blow against the youthful new guard of the *New Left Review*, against their attempt to develop through a new interpretation of English history a distinctive political position on the current conjuncture.

When I read *The Poverty of Theory* in 1978 I saw another 'police action', written with an even more violent fury, and found myself one of those on the receiving end. It is never pleasant to find oneself portrayed as a theoreticist fool rotting the minds of those intellectual incompetents ill-educated enough to listen to one. In 1966 Anderson responded by hitting back hard, exposing Thompson's own politics to systematic critique. Given the violence of the attack his response was justified. I too was determined to hit back hard and did so in the substantive arguments of my review of *The Poverty of Theory* (reprinted as Chapter 4 in this volume). I was equally determined neither to match Thompson's abuse with my own, nor to denigrate those things he had done which I respected. I said: 'It is an urgent necessity that socialists find means to *differ* which do not destroy the wider possibilities of communication.' (p. 58) This urgency is even greater today. Socialists are few, in retreat and face an uncertain future. But Anderson's book has tested this conviction almost to breaking, and it is only by a silence of nearly three years that I now feel able to honour it.

For Anderson's generosity towards Thompson is coupled with a churlish disparagement of myself and Barry Hindess. Alone, of all the Marxists mentioned in this work and in a previous one, *Considerations on Western Marxism*, we are subjected to ridicule and abuse. One should note that it is impossible to find any serious argument which justifies or substantiates this outburst. As a consequence our arguments remain unaddressed and unanswered. Anderson inveighs as follows:

> There can be no doubt that in England a species of spin-off from Althusser's work occurred in the 70s which does answer to some of Thompson's severest strictures. The writings of Hirst, Hindess and their associates notoriously effected a *reductio ad absurdum* of some of Althusser's ideas – before successively rejecting Althusser himself as too empiricist, then their own earlier notions as too rationalist, and finally Marx as too revolutionary. But this weightless iconoclasm, however understandably a provocation to Thompson, has never been part of the mainstream of Althusserian work – which it has expressly renounced, along with Marxism. (*Arguments*, p. 126)

Later Anderson says:

> *The Poverty of Theory* ends with the declaration of a general jehad against Althusserianism – a call to a new War of Religion on the Left. . . . The harmfulness of this style of polemic to the possibilities of rational or comradely communication on the Left can be in no doubt. (*Arguments*, p. 128)

With this latter statement one can only heartily concur. Anderson rightly rejects Thompson's declaration of war against 'enemies to the Left', but makes one exception to this general armistice, myself and Hindess. Presumably he thinks that as we have 'renounced' Marxism we are fair game. Even if this were true, and I shall return to it in a moment, does Anderson want to have hostile and abusive relations with non-Marxist socialists? He would find it difficult if he were to try and deny we are sincere and committed socialists. Anderson's exception to his sensible general rule might strike the reader as irrational and unintelligible. To understand it we must indulge in a little history. The first and probably decisive component of that history is simple; it consists in an essay of mine reprinted as Chapter 5 in this volume called 'The Uniqueness of the West'. That essay could only have antagonised Anderson for it was a sustained critical rejection of the organising problem and theoretical apparatus of his books *Passages from Antiquity to Feudalism* and *Lineages of the Absolutist State*. It could hardly be called a generous review; it hits hard and fails to praise, but it is neither personalist nor abusive. It certainly neglects to praise the breadth of historical scholarship Anderson displays, and the quality and originality of some of the narrative reconstructions of particular national histories. The reason for this is simple; I regarded Anderson as a thinker of some stature, who neither needed mollifying praise nor would shy away from critical comment. If Hindess or I were indeed 'weightless iconoclasts', Anderson's invective would be unnecessary, our triviality and irrelevance would be manifest to all. But clearly the critique must have weighed heavily, for among other things it demonstrated how divergent were Anderson's problems and concepts from any normal construction of Marxism.

It also made reference to a text Anderson might prefer to forget, 'Problems of Socialist Strategy', published in *Towards Socialism*. In itself it is an interesting and forcefully presented piece. But in that essay Anderson made one statement which he certainly would wish to retract today:

> Leninist strategy in the West is fundamentally *regressive*: it threatens to destroy a vital historical creation [democracy – PQH], when the task is to surpass it. . . . Leninism is refused by the whole cultural texture of the advanced capitalist societies of the West. ('Problems', p.230)

Anderson included this in a context of unqualified praise for the uniquely Western political achievement of democracy. In the context of rapprochement with the Labour Party in 1964 this was understandable; now it and the *NLR*'s orientation at that time seem uncomfortably close to the Eurocommunism he excoriates in *Arguments within English Marxism*. Subsequent to 1964 Anderson turned toward the Trotskyism of the Fourth International and to a new estimation of Lenin. He now insists on the necessity, at some

point in the revolutionary process, of a violent overthrow of the
bourgeois state and the construction of new institutions of mass
political power.

I do not regard Anderson's change of heart as absurd, although I
do not sympathise with it, but he clearly seems embarrassed to be
reminded that it has taken place. In *Arguments* he rehearses the
history of his dispute with Thompson and the old *NLR* board,
putting forward a case for the new board's consistency in
addressing certain problems. He is silent on the complexities and
reversals of line, and on *NLR*'s inattention to certain major trends
in Marxism (for which see Sassoon, 'The Silences of *New Left
Review*'). Anderson passes over a good deal in silence, yet his
differences with us surface in short but intense bursts of dismissive
abuse.

Why? My review challenged the theoretical foundations of his
magnum opus. Our remarks on history in *Pre-Capitalist Modes of
Production* likewise challenged his commitment to identifying
Marxist work with a certain type of historical investigation. The
commitment in *Marx's Capital and Capitalism Today* to a root and
branch critique of some of the central doctrines in *Capital* and our
insistence on the centrality of the Labour Party for British Socialists
certainly cannot have prompted him to agree. An index of this
disagreement is that following the writing of the review I was told
by the member of the *NLR* board to whom I had shown it as a
courtesy that the *Review*'s pages were closed to me thereafter. I had
never taken them to be open, and I had not greatly regretted the
fact. The political and theoretical differences between us are vast. I
see no basis for reducing them and no need to call for a bogus
'reconciliation'. At the same time I see no point in pursuing
vendettas. I accept wholeheartedly that certain ways of engaging in
disputes on the Left have been nothing other than destructive. We
must begin not merely to mouth adherence to norms of rational and
comradely communication on the Left but must actually keep to
them.

I shall begin in this respect by clearing the ground and outlining
my own attitude to the *NLR*. I do this for two reasons. One, to
show my commitment to being open and honest about the basis of
one's differences. The other, to dispel the possible assumption that I
have never taken either Anderson or the *NLR* seriously. The reverse
is the case. In the period 1966–8 I was a member of a student

political group at Leicester University which published a magazine called *Sublation* in which *NLR* took a considerable interest. Several members of *Sublation*, myself and Mike Gane in particular, were intellectually and politically close to certain members of the *NLR* board, notably Anthony Barnett and Ben Brewster. Two things broke this limited connection. One was the publication of Althusser by *NLR*; we enthusiastically adopted Althusser's programme of work, whereas after giving it an initial introduction in the UK, many of the board became hostile to it. The other was a large part of the board's growing commitment to Trotskyism, something I frankly admit I do not understand.

The Marxist-Leninist journal *Theoretical Practice* (1971–3), of whose editorial group I, Tony Cutler, Mike Gane, Barry Hindess and Athar Hussain, were among the members, consciously set ourselves the task of avoiding what we saw to be the main failures of the *Review*: its a-political 'culturalism' – winning the English intellectuals to European Marxism, and its failure to establish any political or democratic relation to its own 'constituency'. *TP* sought to be different, to build through study groups and conferences a circle of committed supporters and contributors. Our aspiration was a more open and democratic relation to our constituency. We failed. *TP* exhausted itself in intense and honest, but bitter and irresoluble struggles about the correct line of theoretico-political work. Such is the inevitable fate of any small Marxist sect which sets itself a world-historic task where circumstances defy its accomplishment and whose members are sufficiently clear about elementary political facts not to repeat dogged and irrelevant slogans until and after they become senile. I do not regret *TP*, although it disillusioned and thwarted many of those who believed in it. Its internal mode of discourse accounts for much of the violence of our polemics – fierce about concepts and political positions, but I would say in our defence seldom mean about people.

NLR and *TP* ceased to communicate. Ben Brewster left the *Review* on the immediate issue of their attitude toward China's relations with the Bandaranaike regime. The *Review*'s pages were closed to us and we ceased to have any meaningful personal contacts or discussions. It should be remembered that Anderson's work, along with Sartre's, had been central in my own intellectual formation. 'The Origins' opened my eyes to the possibility of serious Marxist work. We renounced a definite heritage in the break with them. I have no idea whether they had any regrets at our evolution. In 'The Uniqueness of the West' I attempted an assessment of the political strategy of the *NLR* and the role Anderson's work played in providing its theoretical underpinnings down to 1975. This was critical but in my view fair comment. *NLR* did not attempt to engage in dialogue.

To return to Anderson's claims that we have renounced 'the mainstream of Althusserian work, along with Marxism'. This is no less than outrageous. I never developed a direct relation with Althusser and have had only the slightest contact with his circle. This was a matter of choice, for members of the *TP* editorial group did visit Paris to seek such relations and were warmly welcomed. Althusser did not regard *TP* as the product of 'weightless iconoclasts' nor did Balibar, whose 'Self-Criticism' in *TP* 7/8 was in direct response to the probings of Tony Cutler. Likewise, Dominique Lecourt took a close interest in *TP*. I, however, always suspected there was no common situation for political work and that our own independent theoretical work was best served by a definite distance. This being said, I have never 'renounced' Althusser. I have criticised his theories radically but I have always made clear what my critical work owes to its starting point and have never ceased to defend Althusser's enterprise as the most audacious and productive development in Marxist theory since the last World War. Althusser now lies prostrate, his life in ruins and the companion of his adult years killed by his own hand. I have never met the man and yet I feel a profound sorrow for him. To be told I have 'renounced' him is a shabby remark and is undeserved. I have renounced neither him nor his work.

Anderson's 'mainstream' is partly valid and partly curious. I am glad Anderson defends the productivity of Althusserian work against Thompson's ignorant jibes, but his defence is of a 'mainstream', largely confined to those who have 'applied' Althusser's theories in some definite line of research. I have no wish to disparage Poulantzas or Baudelot and Establet, or others. All I will say is that most of the people on Anderson's list have not tried to push forward Althusser's main lines of theoretical work on epistemology or the theory of modes of production. Anderson may not like what we say, and we would accept that it shatters much of the substance of Althusser's theory. But it does attempt to address and re-pose his main problems. To say we are a diversion from the 'mainstream' is, therefore, incongruous.

As to renouncing Marxism, Anderson is not alone in his claims; they are made by Göran Therborn and many others. For them to renounce the 'determination of the economy in the last instance' is to cut the sheet anchor keeping one's position in the Marxist ocean. I admit it is no minor trifling with points of doctrine. However, as I point out in the essays reprinted in this volume, both Thompson in *The Poverty of Theory* and Anderson in *Passages* and *Lineages* have hardly kept to the letter of Marxist theory and have radically modified the role of the economy in historical change. Yet both continue to present themselves as genuine Marxists. We, the authors of *Marx's Capital and Capitalism Today*, at least try to make our relation to Marx open, to clearly map the theoretical differences between Marx and ourselves. If we have been direct in this matter we have had no choice, our very enterprise demands it. Of course, I am not an 'orthodox' Marxist; nobody actually can be one and Marx certainly was not. But I refuse to concede I have 'renounced' Marxism. Such terminology implies leaving a viable enterprise for discreditable political reasons or intellectual confusion. I write at a time when there is no cachet in seeking to hang on to the label 'Marxist' and venial intellectuals are queueing up to disparage socialism.

Marxists have been struggling with trying to square the circle for a long time, trying to make a viable doctrine out of the 'determination of the economy in the last instance' under pressure of theoretical and political necessities. I have struggled hard to confront these theoretical and political necessities, and in doing so I have been led a long way from the words, concepts and political positions of Marx. I have become convinced we *cannot* square the circle and can only ruin ourselves politically and intellectually by continuing in a futile exercise in loyalty to the greatest thinker in the social sciences and the socialist movement.

I *cannot* abandon or renounce the claim to be a Marxist given my theoretical and political position. I will admit to being heterodox and ultra-critical, yes, but I will not accept the charge of ceasing to be a Marxist. My own work makes no sense if I reject what Marx *tried to do* rather than how he did it. I *cannot* renounce the broadest aims Marx set himself, to provide the theoretical basis for a non-utopian socialist politics which would ultimately lead the people of this earth to make a human condition without famines, ignorance, war and oppression. Such a politics cannot wait for revolutions in the advanced Western capitalist countries, the tasks have become too urgent. A large part of the world is starving, the whole world is threatened by senseless and barbarous war. We must make what progress as we can where we can, with such small victories as are attainable to us.

Anderson at the very end of his book says: 'the absence of a truly mass and revolutionary movement in England, as elsewhere in the West, has fixed the perimeter of all possible thought in this period' (*Arguments*, p. 207). Yes, how true. But we live in this period and no other, we must face this fact and not live in the hope of revolutions to come. The British working class is shrinking, fragmented and profoundly unrevolutionary. Anderson knows this and yet he cannot draw *my* conclusions. Edward Thompson at least does not sit waiting for the socialist revolution he dreams of. My democratic socialist politics Anderson may consider a dismal social democratic pragmatism. I do not believe it to be so and I cannot accept his commitment to a 'revolutionary' politics which seems a hopeless abstraction in the current situation. The last line of *Arguments* reads: 'It would be good to leave old quarrels behind, and to explore new problems together.' I shall not repeat the same to him; the intellectual and political differences are too great to pretend that either of us could or would wish to 'explore new problems together.' I shall say something different. Let us pursue our differences rationally, and accept that we fight as socialists, from opposed positions, but on the same side.

Anderson's critique of Thompson

Anderson's attention to Thompson's work goes beyond a reply to *The Poverty of Theory* and involves a major re-assessment of his historical work and political positions. I do not intend to review the whole enterprise here but to concentrate on the salient points I consider especially valuable.

Firstly, Anderson offers a qualified defence of Althusser against the claims of *The Poverty of Theory*. Most impressive is his account of Althusser's theoretical-political career in which he decisively rebuts the charge that Althusser is the intellectual culmination of Stalinism and his work nothing more than 'a straightforward ideological police action' (Thompson, *Poverty*, p. 275). I must admit I thought the charge too absurd to require patient and detailed *political* refutation, and largely ignored Althusser's politics and the French political context of his intervention in my own reply. Anderson's contribution has persuaded me the task was well worth undertaking; it shows that patient historical re-construction of the political context is a valuable complement to the type of theoretical defence of the Althusserian enterprise I offered in 'The Necessity of Theory'.

Secondly, Anderson demonstrates – as I did – Thompson's tendency to equate Marxist investigative practice with historiography *tout court*. Linked to this is a demonstration of the inadequacy of Thompson's central concept of 'experience' and his conception of classes as groups of people who make their history through conscious experience of their nature as a class. Anderson shows that 'experience' is neither a unitary category nor does it always lead to positive and productive knowledge by agents of states of affairs as Thompson supposes. Anderson says: 'Experience as such is a concept *tout azimuts*, which can point in any direction. The self-same events can be lived through by the agents who draw diametrically opposite conclusions from them.' (*Arguments*, pp. 22–9) To reduce classes to bodies of *conscious* agents involves a transformation of the Marxist concept of classes as groups of agents linked by their structural relations to the means of production. Thompson's notion of classes 'making' themselves does involve the corollary that there are not classes until they are made – in which case as Anderson points out classes in the Ancient World or the French peasantry of Marx's *Eighteenth Brumaire* cannot be classes properly so called.

This critical point is pursued through a critical reading of *The Making of the English Working Class*, the main text on which Thompson's reputation is founded. Anderson shows *The Making* rests on three dubious theses:

1 The first Anderson calls 'co-determination', the claim that the English working class 'made itself as much as it was made' and that creative agency has at least an equal place with the conditioning of socio-economic relationships. Anderson shows that this stress on making leads to inattention to the socio-economic context – a failure to consider the crucial sectors of the

Industrial Revolution, to recognise London was *not* an industrial
city, to reflect the political impact of external events, notably the
American and French revolutions, and to record the extent to
which the Napoleonic wars fostered ties of national chauvinism
between the English people and their rulers.
2 The second is the equation of class with class consciousness.
3 The third is the assumption that by 1832 the working class is
substantially 'made', ignoring the decisive political and economic
changes after 1832 – in particular the political collapse of
Chartism by 1850, the rise of the new unionism and a moderate
socialism based on parliamentary representation.

Anderson concludes that on balance as a theorist Althusser is
closer to 'historical materialism':

Althusser's unilateral and remorseless stress on the overpowering
weight of structural necessity in history corresponds more
faithfully to the central tenets of historical materialism, and to
the actual lessons of the scientific study of the past – but at the
price of obscuring the novelty of the modern labour movement
and attenuating the vocation of revolutionary socialism (*Arguments*, p. 58).

The problem I have with this is that Althusser is unable to
incorporate the complexities of political organisation, struggle and
ideology into his determination by structural necessity. This is
nowhere clearer than in the text where he attempts to do so –
'Ideology and "Ideological State Apparatuses"'. Poultanzas likewise repeatedly stood himself on his head trying to resolve this
problem. There is a genuine problem of relating classes as groups of
agents with a relation to the means of production with classes as
social forces, constituted groups of agents which are the outcome of
the complexities of political struggles and institutions. Thompson
has the merit of trying to address classes as social forces, albeit with
disastrous theoretical means which lead him to make them self-
willing 'actors' unified by a common 'consciousness'. Marxism
continues to have a series of largely unresolved problems in the area
of class theory, and it is a mistake to suppose that the obvious
errors of one attempted route to their solution are a vindication of
the alternative route. Hindess and I have attempted to outline the
problems in the Marxist theory of class and to indicate why both

routes are a non-solution. It is unlikely that the issue can be resolved in a general theory, but only through the complexities of contemporary political calculation or historical reconstruction of definite situations.

Thirdly, Anderson shows – as I do – that Thompson's accusation that Althusser equates mode of production and social formation is absurd: it was he and Balibar who introduced the distinction in the first place. Anderson's claim is that Thompson has utterly misread *Capital*, tending to treat it and the *Grundrisse* as a narrowly focused critique of political economy which shares all the defects of that discipline in reducing the development of the complex whole of society to narrowly conceived economic laws.

Two problems arise here. One is that for all Althusser and Balibar's insistence on the distinction they are unable to pursue it rigorously or accomplish anything with it. It is all very well formally to insist that any social formation is a complex articulation of modes of production in which one is dominant. It is another thing to demonstrate *how* this combination answers to the necessities of structural causality, to move far from the abstract determinations of the structure to the concrete situation. It will not do to assume that given enough time and effort an ordered hierarchy of levels of determination can be set up such that we can move without contradiction to the analysis of the specific conditions in any current conjuncture. To his credit Balibar realised this and tried to cope with it, unsuccessfully, in his self-criticism. Self-appointed 'Althusserians' like Lawrence Harris (1978) have still not understood this and continue to believe the problem is one of effort, much like giving enough typewriters to enough monkeys to finally arrive at the collected works of Shakespeare.

The other point is closely connected with the first. Thompson's criticisms of *Capital* and the *Grundrisse* in *The Poverty of Theory* do, despite many errors, score some palpable hits. He partially realises that the reading in *Reading Capital* is not a complete misreading, that Marx's account of the capitalist mode of production does commit him to a necessary generality of effects of the structure such that, if they are taken at face value, they cannot help but be mapped onto concrete conditions. In *Marx's Capital and Capitalism Today* my co-authors and I examine this problem, a convergence between our arguments and his that Thompson fails to note or understand. We do not offer a monist reading of *Capital*, as if its discourse were the emanation of one coherent set of concepts. We point out that this structural necessity is one vital and predominant component of a complex discourse, in which the necessary effects of the mode of production are both affirmed and denied. Our critique of Marx is *not* that mode of production is a general concept and therefore wrong because general concepts *per se* are wrong. Alex Callinicos in *Is there a Future for Marxism?* notes that to some extent Thompson and ourselves are making a similar point, with different methods and toward different conclusions it must be said. But he equates our critique with a rejection of general explanations *per se*. He concludes:

> They do not explain how in this respect the concept of mode of production differs from any other concept. Precisely what concepts do is to set limits, implicitly distinguishing those cases which fall under them from those that do not. (*Is there a Future*, p. 190)

If this were the case my position would be untenable and crazy, since I have been concerned to defend the explanatory value of other general theories, notably Darwin's theory of natural selection (Hirst, *Social Evolution*, Ch. 2 and Hirst and Woolley, *Social Relations*, Ch. 1) and Freud's metapsychology and theory of the neuroses (Hirst and Woolley, Ch. 8). The issue is a very different one, it does not concern the generality of any theory but the mode in which one particular theory generalises its effects. The concept mode of production used in *Capital* cannot specify rigorously those cases which fall under it and those which do not, it has no way of doing so given its forms of internal and necessary effectivity. The discourse of *Capital* does circle endlessly around the problem of necessary general effects and the inability in the conceptualisation of causality to specify the concrete conditions of realisation of those effects. *Capital* both requires and refuses the systematic realisation of the effects of the structure.

Our solution to this problem is a radical one, to reject the concept of mode of production because it *is* the necessary realisation of the structure in states of affairs. Alex Callinicos says:

> If, however, we understand the primacy of the relations of production as heuristic, reductionism is no longer such a

problem. The concept of relations of production may be taken to constitute the heuristic of the Marxist research programme. (*Is there a Future*, p. 193)

I could heartily concur with this *if* what was being proposed were a relatively open-ended 'research programme' as to how definite relations of production are constituted in social formations and in considering concretely how, in a complexity without a pre-given structure, they tend to become the primary element. This is *not* what Callinicos proposes – despite his insistence, intelligently and forcefully, on the dominance of the relations of production, the problematic nature of mode of production as a concept remains largely intact.

It does so remain too in Anderson's formulations, although on a very different basis. Anderson says: '*Without* the construction of a theory of the mode of production in the first instance, any attempt to produce a "unitary knowledge of society" could only have yielded an eclectic interactionism'. (*Arguments*, p. 67) This is correct, and well expressed against Thompson, who does indeed couple the objective of a 'unitary knowledge of society' with a tendency to 'eclectic interactionism' in which culture, experience and human practice predominate over more traditional Marxist accounts of causality. Thompson is indeed led in a non-Marxist direction of stressing 'culture' and class as human collective practice. What Anderson does *not* say is that it is the couple 'unitary knowledge of society'/'eclectic interactionism' which is problematic. It is clearly absurd to seek such a 'unitary knowledge', to conceive society or a social formation as a totality for which there must be a single explanatory scheme appropriate to its nature as a whole, and to conceive that unity as the outcome of a plurality of ad hoc causal factors. We have been charged time and again with this failing, and of course such a project *is* inconsistent. But what we question is precisely this aim of a 'unitary knowledge' – such a knowledge has as its object a totality, answerable to a general explanatory scheme which identifies certain causes as definitive of the whole, as what makes it a whole. We would press two points. The first is that we cannot have a 'unitary knowledge' – Marxism is one of a number of knowledges relevant to social explanations, but which do not have a common object or method. Psychoanalysis, anthropology, aspects of sociology (in so far as it does not consist of

rival theories of totality to that of Marxism), historiography all
have vital roles to play. Marxism cannot be a universal and self-
sufficient social science. The second is that the objects of analysis in
the case of social formations are not unitary objects with a single
necessary structure. They are not a congeries of unrelated parts
either, but the connectedness of their components is a *construction*,
and one which is made out of elements without a pre-structured
identity. Such constructions are made and re-made. Capitalism, and
socialism too, are not pre-structured wholes, but definite patterns
of construction and reconstruction, in which political practice and
political ideology play vital non-pre-given roles.

In this sense I can accord a vital place to the concept of 'relations
of production' as a heuristic, examining the specific construction of
such relations and determining their specific effects. This is an *open*
process of research, but it is not 'eclectic interactionism'. It has no
necessary causality, but equally it is not a dogmatic pluralism.

Anderson proposes another scheme of analysis. He says:

> It is, and must be, the dominant *mode of production* that confers
> fundamental unity on the social formation, allocating their
> objective positions to the classes within it, and distributing the
> agents within each class. (*Arguments*, p. 55)

What underlies this fundamental unity and the process by which
it changes is a distinctive causal schema:

> For far from lacking any explanatory principle of a 'genetic' type,
> Marx's theory conspicuously possesses one – set out with clarity
> and force in the 1859 *Preface*: the thesis that the contradiction
> between the forces and relations of production is the deepest
> spring of long-term historical change. (*Arguments*, p. 81)

Far from it being the fact that this thesis should be rejected as
leading to an unsatisfactory economic determinism, it has now been
decisively vindicated: 'It so happens, in fact, that we now possess a
stringent and persuasive vindication of its role within Marx's
theory, in Cohen's work, whose intellectual force supersedes
virtually all previous discussion.' (*Arguments*, p. 72)

G. A. Cohen's *Karl Marx's Theory of History: A Defence* is an
intelligent and well-argued book but it cannot bear the weight
Anderson asks of it. In Chapter 2 below, I critically examine
Cohen's book and argue that it cannot justify theoretically the

causal primacy of the forces of production. I should add that I am far from alone in this judgment. Alex Callinicos, in *Is there a Future for Marxism?*, says: 'Cohen, therefore, cannot get off square one, and the detailed elaboration of his argument is undermined by the defects involved in its most basic concepts.' (p. 145)

Callinicos argues on the contrary for the primacy of the *relations of production*. Likewise Andrew Levine and Erik Olin Wright, in *NLR* 123, present a strong case against Cohen and in defence of the relations of production. Anderson cites Olin Wright as one of the leading authors in the Althusserian 'mainstream'. It will be clear that I think switching to the primacy of the *relations* and retaining a concept of mode of production as totality is not the answer. But if one is to retain such a concept the case for the primacy of the relations and, therefore, no necessary contradiction with the forces is overwhelming – as Hindess and I argued in *Pre-Capitalist Modes of Production*. Anderson's re-statement of Marxist verities needs a lot more argument and cannot rest on Cohen. Thompson, at least, in this respect is more open on the problems of economic determinism and clearly convinced that Marxism will suffer a death by intellectual arteriosclerosis if it sticks to the letter of the 1859 *Preface*. Anderson's critique of Thompson, for all its virtues, and I have ignored many, cannot be said to do complete justice to Thompson's perception that Marxism and *Capital* do face real problems. He has dealt clearly and fairly with the weaknesses in Thompson's *solutions*, but I wish he would see that doing this does not vindicate the Marx of the 1859 *Preface*.

Anderson, Althusser and epistemology

Althusser receives considerable justice at Anderson's tribunal on the respective merits of Thompson and himself. But there are certain areas where justice is less than done, let alone seen to be done. One of these is Anderson's account and criticisms of his epistemology. He agrees with a great deal of Thompson's criticism in this area and contends, repeating the claim made in an earlier work, *Considerations on Western Marxism*, that 'Althusser's theory of knowledge ... is ... directly tributary to that of Spinoza.' (*Arguments*, p. 6) Alex Callinicos rightly notes the 'oddity' and the unoriginality of this judgment in *Is there a Future for Marxism?* (pp. 230–1). Althusser acknowledges his debt to

Spinoza, and Anderson was hardly original in pointing to it in
Considerations. Callinicos also rightly points out that in his
conception of the knowledge process and his conception of how
such knowledge is tested Althusser owes a far greater debt to
Gaston Bachelard. In *Considerations* Anderson does recognise
Bachelard's influence, with Canguilhem's, but only in passing. To
say of Althusser as Anderson does – 'His theory of knowledge,
disassociated from controls of evidence, is untenably internalist:
above all it lacks any concept of falsification' (*Arguments*, p. 7) – is
less than just, particularly when his debt to Bachelard is recognised.

Althusser's theory of knowledge *is* untenable – as Barry Hindess
and I have argued – but *not* because it is internalist. Althusser is *not*
a falsificationalist, true indeed, but many modern philosophers of
science are not – notably Paul Feyerabend (*Against Method*) and
Ian Hacking ('Language, Truth and Reason') from very different
positions. To be an internalist is *not* to dissociate knowledge from
controls of evidence. Bachelard insists that modern theoretical-
empirical science is 'materialised theory'; it constructs its entities
and experiments but it uses controls and tests. The point is that
there is no extra-theoretical domain of evidence to be the measure
of theory and no common method of demonstration of the validity
of knowledges between the different sciences. Bachelard rejects the
notion of a unitary enterprise called 'science', linked by common
methods. Hence he must reject a single category of 'evidence'; there
are eviden*ces* and they do not function in a falsifying manner.
Evidence is not *given*, it is not extra-theoretical, but it does not
thereby cease to be evidential.

In this context, Anderson castigates Hindess and me for saying
'facts are never given, they are always produced' and agrees that
Thompson condemns us 'with every justification' (*Arguments*, p.
7). In saying this we have never claimed that knowledge is without
controls or tests, rather we have been concerned to argue that
knowledges construct theoretically what they will count as evidence. Sometimes, indeed, they cannot handle what they construct.
Domains of evidentialisation differ. There are *no* brute facts, but
products of knowledge which are assessed by the procedures
knowledges deem proper. Evidentialisation is *not* the comparison
of theory and reality, but a process internal to knowledge. Tests
and controls do not prove the correspondence of thought and
reality, they do not validate or falsify explanatory schemes but

rather presuppose them for their own validity. Evidence is not 'facts', or rather facts count as such because they are produced in knowledges as evidence. One could continue the argument *ad infinitum*: the point is that Anderson dismisses the case we – and others – make as inherently absurd without really arguing hard for his own claim that there are non-theory dependent facts which falsify theories. *If* that is what he is saying.

Althusser may have gone beyond Bachelard's positions in his epistemology but he has never adopted an irrationalist or cavalier position on the content of knowledge. That content may be internalised within knowledge, but for him the process of knowing is, to use Marx's phrase, 'the appropriation of the concrete in thought'. Further he has never shown hostility to the knowledge of the natural sciences. The theory of the generalities may not work – but Althusser is in very good philosophical company in failing to produce a consistent and defensible epistemological doctrine. And insisting on the 'givenness' of facts along with Thompson will not do so either.

There is also little ground for confidence in Anderson's judgments on an epistemology which owes a great deal to Bachelard, for he has continued to produce an amazing misreading of the latter. In 'The Myths of Edward Thompson', *NLR* 35, he placed Bachelard 'within the idealist tradition' (p. 32, n. 98). Again in *Considerations* Bachelard and Canguilhem are characterised as 'idealists' (p. 57). Alexander Koyré might be considered an 'idealist'. Bachelard's poetics might be so considered too perhaps, but his philosophy of science would best be called in his own phrase 'rationalist materialism'. Perhaps this digging up the bones of old essays will be considered unfair, but Anderson's misjudgment remained constant over ten years (1966–76) and has not been retracted.

Anderson also says that: 'Althusser's system wrongly assimilates knowledge to science *tout court*' (*Arguments*, p. 6) and 'For Althusser immediate experience is the universe of illusion – Spinoza's *vaga experentia*, which induces only error. Science alone, founded on a work of conceptual transformation, yields knowledge.' (*Arguments*, p. 57) Althusser does demarcate systematically between science and ideology. He does speak of ideology as '*méconnaissance*' (misrecognition). *But* he does not consider ideology to be either illusion or error. Ideology is the representation of the imaginary relation of men to their conditions of existence.

That imaginary relation is not illusion. What is recognised by subjects through the representation of the imaginary relation is what it is although it cannot be an account of why it is so. It therefore follows that not all knowledges are science; some knowledges do not penetrate to the determinations of what it is they know but what they know is not false. Althusser treats *theoretical* ideologies as knowledges. So there can be no question of him equating science and knowledge.

Ideology is essential to the conduct of the affairs of men. No society – communism included – can live by science alone. The reason is that no society – as a society – is reducible to a human practice based upon the cognition of its structural determinations. Human persons are subjects, not reasoning engines. Psychic life and social relations involve the constitution of relations *between subjects* and not merely the structural relations that pertain between economic agents. People need to be motivated, consoled, to find a medium for resolving their differences. Ideologies therefore can be productive knowledges essential to an aspect of human conduct. Althusser's insistence on ideology in a communist society should show that he does not regard it as a wholly negative phenomenon. He does challenge, however, the idea that society will one day be subject to the teleology of rational human wills.

Althusser tries to do something powerful and valuable in constructing his theory of ideology; it is subverted by his insistence on the science-ideology couple and on his demand that ideology reproduce the relations of production in such a way that the totality functions as a viable lived society. I have criticised Althusser's theory of ideology, but have always insisted that for Althusser it does not consist in falsity and error. I cannot comprehend how Anderson can make the claim that it does. Clearly, he wants to say that there are facts, objective and non-theoretical, and that men can know them without obscure self-validating sciences that defy experience. Althusser denies this and powerfully. What Anderson wants to say is in my view mistaken but he does not help his case in saying it by misreading Althusser. In this respect – on the theory-independent nature of the facts of historical knowledge – Anderson seems to be at one with Thompson and to misread Althusser in a very similar way.

Anderson appears in part to subscribe to a falsificationalist view but he also indicates that this is not tenable pure and simple. He notes, on p. 12 of *Arguments*, Imre Lakatos's critique of Karl Popper. Marxism is, it would appear, a Lakatosian 'research programme' in which evidence does matter but in which ultimately the value of the programme depends on its capacity, as theory and investigation, to produce new additions to knowledge. For Anderson, Marxism would appear to be a progressive rather than a degenerating 'research programme' – its survival to be measured by its general productivity in producing new knowledge rather than any specific instances of disconfirmation of some of its predictions. I would add two comments here. One is that Lakatos's philosophy of science is also in an important sense 'internalist' – the accumulation of negative evidence is not a reason in itself for the abandonment of a 'research programme'. The other, to which I will return, is that Lakatos's theory is far from strongly legislative, it amounts to a conceptual framework for making sense of the history of science. However, I do not think it sufficiently rigorous to decide one way or the other on Marxism – Lakatos would no doubt have given a less than positive answer. One can say Marxism is progressive or one can say it remains immobilised in the attempts to stave off the contradictions in its theoretical core. I would say that both answers are possible because Marxism has tended to appear productive against many other theories in the social sciences which are moribund and defective. I would also say that many Marxists *have* produced good and innovative analyses – Anderson and Thompson included – whilst straying far from the letter of Marx's methods and concepts. How far these analyses exemplify the 'research programme' is open to question, and with it the role of this concept as a measure of Marxism's productivity. The same is true of Marx himself. So often one is astounded he could produce what he did *when* he did. But if the 1859 *Preface* or certain aspects of *Capital* such as the theory are of value to constitute the core elements of the theory then the answer would surely be that Marxism has either been diverging from that core, doing something else, or degenerating in an attempt to ad hoc away its contradictions.

I do not think Lakatos can help us. The notion of a progressive 'research programme' shuffles away the accumulating theoretical difficulties. If Marxism were not so politically consequential this could be lived with. But conceptual problems do have political consequences – mediately but important none the less. Reconstructing Marxist theory is not to make it consistent, elegant or whatever, but to help us understand what to do politically and how to avoid falling into mistaken judgments and false hopes. Anderson agrees that Marxist theory should be a vital guide to political action and not simply another social science. I wish he could see how necessary are the radical reconstructions we must make if we are to understand and act in the contemporary political situation. Our politics and our estimations of theory differ radically. And so I doubt we can find common ground. It is a pity he cannot accord the same genuineness and sincerity of purpose to my enterprise that I do to his.

Interestingly enough Anderson is not alone in trying to use Lakatos's philosophy of science to defend Marxism as a going concern. Alex Callinicos, a pupil of Lakatos, does this in a more elaborate way than Anderson in *Is there a Future for Marxism?*

Firstly some preliminaries. Lakatos's theory is to be coupled with Alfred Tarski's semantic theory of truth. Thus for the sentence – 'grass is green' – to be true it is necessary that the state of affairs postulated in the sentence be the case. The sentence is true if and only if grass is green. Such a sentence refers to a non-semantic world of objects. Tarski's theory does provide, according to Callinicos, an account of truth as correspondence with an extra linguistic reality. The argument that the entities to which language refers are constituted in, and by it, 'does not alter the fact that discourses do constantly posit the existence of entities external to them to which they refer' (*Is there a Future*, p. 177). The reason for this is that:

> one constitutive feature of language is the constant reaching out to a reality outside it. This feature can only be explained by the fact that there *is* such a reality, and that human beings and their discourse are dependent and subordinate aspects of this reality. (*ibid.*)

This is to stray some way from Tarski and is exactly like the very bad argument of Roy Bhaskar which Callinicos himself condemns on p. 245. Bhaskar claims that the fact that our experiments 'work', that knowledge *is* possible, proves materialism or naturalism, because our experiments correspond to mechanisms in nature which enable this production of knowledge to happen. This is simply circular reasoning. Callinicos is similarly claiming that language refers and reference 'works' because there really is a reality which causes this to happen. Of course, discourses refer to extra-discursive entities. This reaching to a reference outside language in no way justifies the claim that there *is* a single reality outside language, any more than the fact that religions and theologies refer to God justifies the claim there *is* a God. Discourses do refer to extra-discursive entities, quite so, but they refer to entities with the most diverse attributes, not one 'reality'. Discourses can refer to extra-discursive entities like God, purity of heart, soap, and photons. To return to Tarski, the crucial question is not can we semanticise truth, but how do we find out if grass is indeed green? Tarski cannot provide a general means for determining states of affairs nor need he, and there is no reason to suppose our means in one area – common sense, 'It looks green to me' – will match up with our means in quite different areas like physics. Tarski's definition concerns the truth of propositions; what it cannot prove is the knowledge claims made in them. That must be done outside philosophy; *how* it is done is properly not Tarski's concern. Tarski's definition is not an epistemology. Callinicos knows this and, therefore, seeks to add to it a set of criteria whereby we can tell not merely whether knowledges determine states of affairs validly or not, according to their own standards of validity, but whether those knowledges correspond to reality and how and why their standards of validity enable them to do so.

Callinicos accepts that 'Hindess and Hirst's critique of epistemology does highlight the dogmatic dangers involved in insisting that all scientific statements conform to some set of principles which have a privileged relation to reality' (*Is there a Future*, p. 180), and concludes that: 'the way round this problem can only be a theory of immanent rationality. In other words, theoretical discourses must be evaluated in terms of their degree of success in resolving the problems they set themselves.' (*ibid.*) Now in itself there is nothing pernicious in such a theory – Lakatos does indeed offer rigorous reconstructions of scientific change. But as Callinicos is aware this is not an epistemology properly so called. He accepts that two theses need to be added to it to transform it 'into a full-blooded epistemology' (*ibid.*, p. 184). These are 'metaphysical realism' – the belief in a real world prior to and independent of thought and governed by natural laws, and 'epistemological optimism' – the belief that those laws are accessible to knowledge and we can provide an adequate account of them. These two theses – subscribed to by Lakatos at a much earlier date – apparently provide the underpinnings to convert the methodology of scientific research programmes into an epistemology. This epistemology 'not only provides objective criteria for the evaluation of discourses but in so doing relates them to the regulation of the truth' (*ibid.*, p. 184). The criteria of progress or degeneration, taken from Lakatos's methodology, 'must be taken as the means through which their degree of approximation to the truth is established' (*ibid.*). The problem with this is that progress or degeneration in Lakatos's methodology are evaluated relative to the explanatory theory, *not* by correspondence with reality. Lakatos's 'methodology' in no sense proves or justifies the theses of metaphysical realism and epistemological optimism, nor does it strictly require them. It is the desire to have an epistemology which leads Callinicos to claim they underpin Lakatos's position. If they do so, they are in grave need of underpinning themselves.

History

Althusser also receives less than full justice in Anderson's treatment of his account of historical time. Althusser's treatment is part of his critique of the couple humanism-historicism. He is concerned to demonstrate how the concept of expressive totality, in which every part mirrors the essence of the whole, is related to the conception of history as a whole formed of successive teleologically developing expressive totalities. Time is a double essential section: each part reflects the presence of the whole in temporality and this co-presence of the parts in the whole is mapped onto chronological time, the time in which the teleological process of history reveals itself. The essential section is the double presence of the subject which makes history; each totality is the emanation of a subject and the whole process of historical development is the presence-in-becoming of the subject which underlies and motivates it. In 'The Necessity of Theory' I have shown how Thompson's conception of 'historical materialism' exemplifies this couple humanism-historicism.

Althusser wanted to argue that a complex totality had no such essential section, that it is a complex of differential temporalities which are reducible to no moment of presence. Anderson claims that this concept of differential times is taken from the *Annales* school of historians, from Braudel and Labrousse. What he does therefore is to reduce the concept of differential times of the structure to differential empirical periodicities (*Arguments*, pp. 73–4). He goes on to identify 'the true weakness of Althusser's discussions of history': 'not his emphasis on the existence of different sectoral times, which was salutary, but his failure to stress the necessity of reconvening them within a plenary societal time' (*Arguments*, p. 75). This 'weakness' is nothing of the kind, it is the primary object of Althusser's criticism. Althusser wants to deny such a 'plenary societal time' because such a plenum is nothing but the co-presence of the moments of a totality. Althusser is guilty of a 'grave confusion' because he does not realise that chronological time is the essential measure of historicity: 'Time as *chronology* is a single, homogeneous continuum. There is nothing in the least "ideological" about this concept of temporality, which forms the scientific object of such institutions as the Greenwich Observatory.' (*Arguments*, p. 75) No, there is nothing in the least ideological about it if one is content to look at one's watch. What *is* problematic is the identification of such time with a single historical process, in which the plenum of societal time forms part of the plenum of the one great movement in which history is made and which is identified with chronological time. This identification makes history both a story and a teleology, a process of becoming and fulfilment 'of' something. Anderson admits this when he says: 'The *relevant* time in which all regional histories should be convened is not an empty grid of dates, but the full movement of the social formation as a whole.' (*Arguments*, p. 75) Indeed! An empty grid of dates can be left to antiquarians, what is of interest is the nature and direction of this 'movement' which takes place within the grid. It is the 'movement' Althusser wishes to problematise, not the grid – the grid is merely one of its supports. The combination of movement and grid makes possible a necessary 'story'.

Anderson's history with a plenum of societal time and a movement of the social formation as a whole is a historicism. In G. A. Cohen's version of Marx it is the history of man's making himself through the process of development of the productive forces. It is history *with* a subject – a secularised and reduced sub-Hegelian teleology.

Now Althusser's attempt to construct *another history*, a theoretical history which appropriates the concrete through concepts which do not reflect the immediate properties of its objects, is a failure – as Hindess and I have shown in the Conclusion to *Pre-Capitalist Modes of Production*. The answer is not to produce another philosophy of history but to abandon the enterprise – to give up seeking to rationalise as necessity a teleological *story*. I accept that our Conclusion is over-polemical and appears to stress, along with the problematicity of such an enterprise, the impossibility of historiography. It was written to demonstrate the defects of Marxism when identified with a 'science of history' but has been misread as an attack on historical writing *per se*. But it is right to argue against an attempt to identify the fulfilment of a single 'process' in a succession of interpenetrating plenary times.

Anderson is correct to challenge Thompson's use of history as a 'pattern book of moral examples' (*Arguments*, p. 85). But at least Thompson's position has one great advantage, the philosophical defence of the relevance of knowledge of the past; it treats history as a whole as made by men. What links past and present, what makes the past relevant, is that it can speak to us as we too are engaged in 'making'. Thompson is a rigorous historicist. What links past and present is experience, values and their bearing on present purposes. Anderson asserts, on the contrary:

> The continuity of past and present is thereby supposed at the
> basic level where it is materially effective – in the objective
> processes of societal development and change, which till now has
> *not* – precisely – been the arena of a celebration of free collective
> agency. (*ibid.*)

For Anderson it is necessary to stress the '*past*, which lies beyond any material alteration by the activities of the present' and is the 'essential object of knowledge for Marxism' (*ibid.*). The continuity 'between past and present . . . is necessarily causal' (*ibid.*). Now Thompson can say that our judgments about the past, while they can alter nothing in the past, may change everything, for our judgments may change the way we act. Past and present are linked *in the present* by how we judge and value men's actions in the past and how we act on the judgments. Thompson can marshal some impressive philosophical support for his view, notably R. G. Collingwood.

It is less easy to justify Anderson's view. Ultimately, Anderson's *causal* link between past and present is either a misuse of terms or something much less dramatic, which does not justify the *whole* past being the 'essential object' of Marxist knowledge. For the whole past to be such an essential object it must be a unity and for that unity to be causal, past causes must either reverberate today or the same causes must act today as they did in the past. Now it is a simple matter of logic that *past* events cannot causally effect subsequent ones. If something at T.1 is purported to have effects at T.2 and has disappeared in the meantime then those effects at T.2 must carry the causing components at T.1 with them. The causing components should therefore be observable at T.2 The notion of a *causal* link between past and present is a misuse of language. How therefore can past causes reverberate today? In no way except by being reproduced today – they are currently observable and in no wise specially 'historical'. Likewise to say that the same causes act today as in the past may well be true, and we may gain by considering their previous action – in this respect the study of history is not 'valueless' as we recklessly claimed. However, if one means by this something like the doctrine of causality that underlies G. A. Cohen's account of historical development as the eventuation of the development of the forces of production we have every reason to question it. For it makes history a single process of development *of* something, a process with a subject, and a continuously acting cause connected to the attributes of that subject which leads through successive stages of development to a final outcome in a state of affairs. An outcome perhaps not essentially necessary as our immanent becoming, but nevertheless the conclusion of a single motivated chain of events going somewhere and linked by a single subject that underlies its unity as a process. This is philosophy of history in the bad sense, a sub-Hegelian teleology without the essential immanence of the unfolding of potentiality, but unified as the purposive practice of a single subject.

If we argue that some forms of reproduction of causes do exist and that some causes do act today as in the past we have conditional grounds for the value of historiography, the rigorous study of records. What we do not have is a general licence to regard the *whole* past as an 'essential object' *because* of its causal consequences. Bits of it will be simply irrelevant. Likewise we have no reason to regard the history of humanity as a single 'story'; for a long part of that history it consists of different and mutually irrelevant stories. The unification of the contemporary world, in which we all live within a few minutes of mutual destruction, should not mislead us in this matter. However, as I shall show, this very *difference*, the absence of a single 'story', while it undermines the role of a certain historiography – identified with teleological philosophy of history – does create a vital role for another. I admit that my commitment to anti-historicism led me to argue in such a way that my position could be read as the outcome of an anti-historiographical prejudice. I do not regret, however, one of the benefits of that anti-historicism, the rejection of the whole human past as the 'essential object' of Marxist knowledge, and the ability to recognise that Marxism is not privileged as historiography. Thompson's identification of Marxism with historiography is pernicious, but so is Anderson's identification of it with a general causal theory of historical development. He *is* closer to Marx in this matter than I am, but I am convinced it is a propinquity not to be celebrated. The opposition is not one between a general theory of history and a 'sociology of revolution' (*Arguments*, p. 85) obsessed with the present. This is a false opposition, if historiography has a value it is not as part of, or in opposition to, such a 'sociology of revolution'.

If historiography has a genuine value as a form of knowledge it is not one unique to it or which qualifies its position as the Queen of the Sciences, as in Thompson's hyperbolic judgment. If, as I have said, the histories of the human race do not form a single 'story' then what they offer are various domains of difference, different ways of being human persons and different forms of culture and social life which do not form the branches of a single developmental tree. Historiography offers us one way of decomposing that bogus unity 'man' – in the neuter sense of *Mensch* – of overthrowing the commitment to the bogus side of Enlightenment humanism to which Marxism has been the primary and unfortunate legatee. For what records offer us is a domain in which we can reconstruct forms of human existence in which we cannot easily recognise ourselves and in which mirror of differences we may glimpse some shreds of understanding of what we *are*.

Historiography is not alone in this. Anthropology and psychoanalysis offer other and equally powerful registers of difference, not merely the difference of the exotic, but in psychoanalysis the knowledge that we are not a simple undivided something, that we are not at one with ourselves. The historiography which offers this is not solely a *Marxist* historiography – as Anderson who has the great merit of taking non-Marxist historians seriously should be the first to recognise. If we have a great debt to historical writing it is primarily to the new intellectual and social history which has done so much to explore such difference, to the work of writers such as Keith Thomas, Frances Yates and D. P. Walker in the sphere of intellectual history and Alan MacFarlane, H. C. Erik Midelfort, and Natalie Zemon Davies in social history. Norman Cohn spans both provinces in a remarkable way. In working on the role of magic in the history of the scientific revolution and on the history of the European 'witch craze', I have come to see how much historiography has to offer.

What it has to offer is in no sense the reconstruction of 'the full movement of the social formation of a whole' in its 'plenary societal time'. Nor is it specially in the field of 'explanation' (*Arguments*, p. 99) that historiography has an important contribution to make. If anything its contribution lies in dealing with ideas, events and persons that virtually defy explanation; in settling with explanatory accounts which have all too easily brushed such things aside. Where historiography has most to contribute is in rebutting the idea that so much of human thought and action is nothing more than a 'freak', a byway on our history of reason. Thompson, who specialises in his own species of recovery with some distinction, can nevertheless say: 'after all to the rational mind, the greater part of the history of ideas is the history of freaks' (*Poverty*, p. 195). The best historical writing offers a way to make this triumphalist self-consciousness, this naive self-possession of the 'rational mind', giddy. The object is not to celebrate irrationalism, but to lead us to a knowledge of the perils of rationalism.

In this respect philosophies of history like R. G. Collingwood's or practices of historical writing like E. P. Thompson's have something going for them which escapes Anderson's strictures. If they are shorn of the historicist assumptions that history is one province of human making, then their stress that historical writing is the recovery of past significances by present judgments has much to commend it. Historical writing must be centred in the present, in the concerns of the present. If it does not consist merely in the vindication of our own views of ourselves or in triumphalist accounts of modernity, it is because some historians can recognise that the past *is* different, not merely an earlier stage of our 'story', but a means of unsettling ourselves and investigating, however partially, what we *are*. Historical writing is neither valueless as knowledge nor politically valueless. Those words in the Conclusion to *Pre-Capitalist Modes of Production* have been read out of their context; it was not to all knowledges that historical writing was held to have no inherent value, but to a highly particular conception of Marxist-Leninist politics and theory. Even then it was not historical writing *per se* that was rejected, but rather such writing when it did not serve to aid the analysis of the current situation. My politics have changed, not my view of history. Changing political concerns mean a change in the value and relevance of types of historical work. But what is valuable is not a 'science of history', or 'historical materialism' as a philosophy of history, and certainly not history for history's sake. When Marxists have made a contribution to historical writing it is not in this guise. If historiography is relevant to politics, it is not to the kind of militant Marxist-Leninist politics I once espoused. That politics cannot accept ambiguities, absurdities, lost causes or the existence of human evil – except as lessons in its morality play or as heroic failures to be celebrated as we make the triumphs to come. Only another kind of politics – aware of human evil and buoyed-up by no crass revolutionary hopes – can hope to draw from historical writing some shreds of wisdom.

Chapter 2

G. A. Cohen's Theory of History

Karl Marx's Theory of History: A Defence has received widespread praise as a rigorous attempt to reassert the validity of traditional 'historical materialism' against fashionable attempts to re-define Marxism in order to remove the incubus of technologism and economic determinism. It offers a sustained reading of the central texts of Marx using the techniques of modern analytical philosophy. Cohen believes modern philosophical methods enable us to re-state Marx's materialism according to new standards of clarity and analytic rigour such that it becomes a defensible doctrine. Cohen faces two ways in this defensive operation: on the one hand, against non-Marxist critics like H. B. Acton and J. Plamenatz who have attempted to use Anglo-Saxon philosophical methods to demonstrate the fundamental weaknesses of 'historical materialism'; and on the other hand, against Marxist theorists like Althusser and his various followers who have attempted to assert the primacy of the relations of production over the forces of production, to define the 'instances' of the mode of production as relatively autonomous and to conceive the 'determination of the economy in the last instance' as an 'overdetermined' process reflecting the complex structure of the social whole.

Cohen makes a strong case for Marx's insistence on the dominance of the productive forces, something that is by no means peculiar to him being strongly argued on exegetical grounds by W. H. Shaw and as part of a theoretical critique by my co-authors and me in *Marx's Capital and Capitalism Today*. Cohen assumes that Marx's position on the dominance of the forces of production is part of a coherent theory, whereas we have tried to show that it is

part of a highly ambivalent and contradictory complex discourse in
which this primacy is both asserted and must be denied. Cohen can
make this assumption because his method of reading involves the
systematic *reconstruction* of Marx's discourse into a series of
simple interrelated empirical propositions. This is not the way
Marx wrote *Capital*, and with good reason. Marx has a conception
of the special methods of investigation and presentation appropriate to capitalism as a complex totality. Marx is not a precursor of
modern positivism who unfortunately lacked the means to present
his propositions clearly. In choosing a method very different to
Marx's own, Cohen is forced to set on one side certain of the
central substantive results of Marx's own method and his conception of the process of producing knowledge.

Hegel, Marx and the totality

The first sign of the effect of Cohen's own choice of method in
reconstructing Marx becomes clear in his account of Hegel. His
account seeks to make Hegel reasonable and intelligible, and it
succeeds quite well in making aspects of Hegel's philosophy clear
and purging the impression of Hegel as a cloudy metaphysician
common among those committed to the analytical methods Cohen
uses. Hegel appears as a rational and sensible philosopher such that
we can see why the Marx Cohen constructs could take him
seriously. Cohen's Hegel, however, amounts to an edited reading of
The Philosophy of History. Edited out of Hegel is the Absolute
Idea, and the Absolute Spirit; in consequence Hegel's conception of
history as *part* of a process whereby the totality realises its essence
in dialectical development through contradiction is elided. History
becomes a succession of incarnations of spirit in particular peoples,
in national characters, but *what* presides over these successive
incarnations is lost. Hegel is a systematically religious thinker – a
formidable logician, well-informed about developments in contemporary history, natural science, economics and psychology –
but nevertheless a Christian metaphysician, albeit of an unorthodox cast. Cohen's history is the realisation of subjectivity at
higher and higher levels of self-consciousness and freedom. But for
Hegel history, as Althusser contends, is a process *without a subject*;
subjects are part of its process, but the Absolute Idea and the

Absolute Spirit is *not* a subject, it is beyond subjectivity in the sense of agency or personality. It is a process of immanent becoming without a finite end or historical goal, and Marx in secularising Hegel reduces Hegel's dialectic to a definite historical process – the realisation of the potential of humanity, its development through contradiction and conflict toward harmonious self-fulfilment in communism. The Hegelian dialectic is operative in history but is not merely the dialectic of history. Althusser, in correctly identifying Hegel's conception as a 'process without a subject', falsely supposes this conception to be transferable to Marx. It cannot be transferred without retention of the Absolute Idea and that idea cannot be made compatible with *any* version of materialism.

Even so, Marx's theory is more faithful to Hegel than Cohen's, for if humanity is the subject of history its development proceeds through the contradictory movement of a series of social totalities. Mode of production for Marx is a totality and not an assemblage of externally related parts. Cohen in asserting the primacy of the forces of production must disarticulate these totalities, reducing the social whole to a series of discrete components causally related through relations of functional dependence and entailment. This is not an illusion; Marx does, indeed, must do this in asserting the primacy of the forces of production. They must be external to the relations they cause to arise and be overthrown. Marx, however, ties this conception of primacy into a scheme of the contradictory development of social wholes, each of which is a form of society and a stage of realisation of humanity's potential. He is thereby saddled with a contradiction between the conception of primacy and the successive totalities for which it serves as a motor, between the motor of the process and the form of the process. This leads him both to assert *and* to deny primacy, both to maintain a necessary evolution of the historical process toward realisation and to subvert it, both to posit humanity as a subject underlying historical development and in his later texts to fail to give any systematic grounding to the status of that capacity to develop. We have analysed these contradictory components of Marx's discourse in *Marx's Capital and Marxism Today*. In seeking to turn Marx's discourse into a set of clear and interrelated propositions Cohen must suppress this complexity and problematicity.

The couple material social

Cohen's silence on the concept of totality is a necessary one. In order to assert the causal primacy of the forces of production and the functional dependence of the relations, he must make the two external one to another, such that the former acts upon the latter. He does this by an ontological distinction, the forces of production are *material* and the relations of production *social*. Cohen distinguishes between the *content* and *form* of a society:

> People and productive forces comprise its *material content*, a content endowed by production relations with *social form*. On entering production relations, persons and productive forces receive the imprint of the form these relations constitute. (*Marx's Theory of History*, p. 89)

The production relations consist in forms of effective possession by social agents of the productive forces. The attributes of persons and the components of the productive forces subsist whatever the social form in which they are contained:

> Being capital and being a slave are . . . relational properties of means of production and men. More specifically, they are social relational properties, whereas being means of production and being a man are not. The latter are possessed independently of social form. (p. 90)

Cohen insists that:

> the technical or material conditions relating man with nature do not, strictly conceived, include relations between men. But while material conditions do not include social relations, they do include some relations between men for not all relations between men are social. (p. 93)

Cohen then proceeds to offer his means of systematically demarcating 'the material from the social situation' and the criterion is that: 'a description is social if and only if it entails an ascription to persons – specified or unspecified – of rights or powers *vis-à-vis* other men' (p. 94).

What we are to make of this differentiation material/social and the criterion for it? To begin with the criterion. It can stand if we take it to be no more than a perverse use of the word 'social'. Cohen can choose to name his demarcated terms 'social' and 'material' or 'alpha' and 'omega' – nothing much is gained or lost thereby. But the criterion purports to distinguish two classes of *entities*, different in nature. In what does this difference, names apart, consist? In a number of propositions:

1 that an objective description of the material forces and men in their material aspect is possible without admixture of terms from relations of possession or 'social' beliefs and ideologies connected with them.
2 that these forces and men thus described are at a certain stage of their independent 'material' development compatible with some other set of 'social' relations other than these under which they have heretofore subsisted.

Let us examine these propositions in turn. The first reminds us of Weber's notion that a strictly objective description of the components of social life is possible prior to the determination of the meaning of these relations. Weber wishes to say that such a description is possible; money, for example, is a golden disc passing from hand to hand. His point, however, is that this will not take us very far in either understanding or accounting for social life without reference to the subjective meaning of the actors. Peter Winch reiterates Weber's point in *The Idea of a Social Science*, taking the example of a game. Now one need not be a Weberian to take this point; for 'subjective meaning' one may substitute categories like beliefs and attributes acquired in social relations.

Cohen may wish to argue that he does not mean *all* social relations but merely *property* relations or relations of effective possession as an extra-legal fact. However, he does not offer a criterion whereby we may distinguish possession relations and *other* social relations; his demarcation is material/social. And clearly this latter opposition *is* consequential; material relations can be abstracted analytically and described objectively. Cohen wishes to say that 'being a man' or the nature of 'productive forces' can be described non-relationally. Technical or material relations to 'nature' as such can be described independent of 'relations between men'.

We can describe a member of the species homo sapiens as a type of animal with certain attributes, an opposable thumb, an erect posture, a brain of a certain range of cubic capacity. . . . But that is *not* a 'man'. Such an animal can be mute, without social relations, and feed like a monkey. A 'man' can only be specified by socially acquired attributes and these in turn will require reference to beliefs. Such attributes and beliefs differ, and with them what it means to be a 'man' – or a woman for that matter.

Is the case of 'productive forces' easier? Cohen says:

> Whether an item is a productive force depends not on its ontology (how physical *it* is), but on whether it contributes to production in virtue of the material character of production. Productively relevant scientific knowledge does pertain to the material task to be performed, and therefore is a productive force. (p. 47)

Production is *material* even if it involves non-physical components like scientific knowledge, and presumably where this is consequential to production, unscientific *belief*, for example, the classificatory schemes which underlie the pharmacopeias of primitive peoples or which explain why they choose to hunt and eat this animal and not that. Cohen never faces up to the challenge of exploring the couple physical-material. Production *must* be material, but can it be non-physical? Cohen must eliminate *magical* attempts to obtain control over phenomena, whether existent or not in our terms, as illusions, however much of the labour-time of society they may consume. But how can he deal with the complex of commodities offered in modern society, operatic performances, faith-healing, vacations, etc.? By specifying a material and non-material component? Almost anything can be said to be 'material'. Cohen will get into the self-same difficulties as Poulantzas in *Classes in Contemporary Capitalism* when he tries to restrict the working class to producers of *material* commodities. If Cohen adopts a generous definition of the productive forces on the model of his admission of scientific knowledge he will be forced to admit to the 'productive forces' beliefs and activities bearing only the most marginal analogy to 'material' production. Further, these beliefs and activities depend on relational properties, on human interaction mediated by custom and language. If this is not 'social' he can keep the word. And if these beliefs and activities are not implicated with the relations of production then the influence of those having the means to direct society's productive power through effective possession is so slight that 'historical materialism' hardly amounts to much.

Cohen has included applied science in the productive forces but his position on managerial skills and the organisation of the division of labour is complex and ambivalent. Science can presumably be treated as socially neutral technical knowledge. 'Work relations' are 'material relations of production' (p. 112) and as such are not part of the economic structure, which is concerned solely with relations of effective possession. Work relations are not productive forces. Cohen says:

> On our account, knowledge of ways of organising labour is a productive force, part of managerial labour power, but the relations established when that knowledge is implemented are not productive forces. It is necessary to distinguish the blueprint for a set of relations from the relations themselves, and it is the first which is a productive force. A principle for allocating tasks in a certain fashion is *used* in production, and it is owned by whomever owns the labour power which includes knowledge of it. Relations obtaining when tasks are divided as it prescribes are neither used nor owned. (pp. 113–14)

Cohen must maintain a description of the production relations limited to effective possession. He must thus differentiate managerial knowledge from its *use*, differentiate content and application. Knowledge, whether scientific or managerial, must be socially neutral in content, part of the material order of social life.

This leads us to the second of Cohen's propositions. To make the forces compatible with successive production relations, such that one set of relations can be overthrown when it is functionally necessary for the productive forces for this to happen, they must be autonomous from the relations. Like science they are a socially neutral *content* with an independent dynamic. One would have liked to have seen some *argument* for this proposition but it is difficult to find it. Time and again one is convinced by the weight of evidence that production techniques, ways of working and knowledges in modern capitalism are not autonomous in their basic character from production for profit on the market. Marx in *Capital* repeatedly gives insightful analyses of the ways in which capitalist relations of production subsume both the labour process and technique. The notion that *existing* large-scale industry, because it is increasingly *socialised*, can be made *socialist* is to be found affirmed and denied in the writings of Marx and Engels. The thesis of the primacy of the forces over the relations leads compulsively toward it, as my collaborators and I have shown in *Marx's Capital and Capitalism Today*. Cohen may wish to say that it is the *potential* inherent in the forces which can be separated from the production relations, that what we should look to is a kind of 'blueprint' overlain by distortions arising from the retarding effects of obsolete production relations. But that would be to accord a much larger influence to production relations than he does, and it would reduce the materiality of the forces such that their causal primacy is difficult to account for. It would amount to saying that given our accumulated knowledge we could do things better if production were not organised for profit, but that in order to do so we would have to scrap the bulk of the organisation of production and production technique. Not quite what Cohen intended to mean, I think, and only true if an important rider is true, that we have available techniques for running a socialist economy such that it would perform better than a capitalist one. Cohen's naivety in this matter is self-evident when he argues that capitalism's development of the forces of production creates the quantitative pre-conditions for socialism, 'a massive surplus', but also its qualitative conditions. Socialism

> also has qualitative prerequisites, and they too, according to Marx, need to be created by capitalism. Capitalism collectivises the working class. . . . It engenders in the working class a cohesion and sophistication, without which democratic self-government would be difficult. . . . What is more, the concentration of wealth under capitalism means that the collective appropriation of the means of production by the producers is easy to achieve, and the struggle against capital forges a unity across the working class which is a desideratum for the political success of socialism. (pp. 214–15)

These words chill me; nothing could be further from the truth – 'capitalism' does nothing of the kind. Those who argue for the dominating role of the relations of production, their *social primacy*, can at least explain why the 'collective appropriation of the means of production' is *not* 'easy to achieve', why the working people are as divided and demoralised as they have ever been, and why we are no nearer the illusory goal of 'abundance' than we were one hundred years ago when Marx died.

Cohen describes the rise of communist society as the 'conquest of form by matter' (p. 129). He goes on to say: 'activity under communism, both within and outside its economy, is not unstructured, but it is not pre-structured. One might say: *the form is now just the boundary created by matter itself*' (p. 131). The couple material/social wreaks its full vengeance: 'It is no great exaggeration to say that Marx's freely associated individuals constitute an alternative to, not a form of society.' (p. 133) Communism is a naturalisation of human relations. We can see the work the couple material/social is set up to do, to create the space for a 'society' without social constraints limited only by man's interaction with the natural world and his own natural and harmonious self-development. The providential end to history Marx plucked from Hegel's metaphysical system is restored, if by the most dubious and problematic means. In a period when the question before serious democratic socialists is how to *organise* a socialist society such that it offers material benefits at least as great as those of capitalism and without a serious loss of political freedom, this must appear not merely unhelpful but a disastrous diversion of theory from pressing political tasks. Cohen's materialism is linked to, set up to produce, an idealised vision of the future.

Cohen's defence of the primacy thesis

Cohen correctly distinguishes between showing that Marx argued for the causal primacy of the forces of production and proving that that thesis is right. He does show that Marx did so argue, ignoring the fact that he also argued the opposite, and failing to explain why Marx should equivocate in this way. His proof of primacy is contained in three propositions: 'Men are in a respect to be specified somewhat rational. The historical situation is one of scarcity. Men possess intelligence of a kind and degree which enables them to improve their situation.' (p. 162)

Let us begin with the second proposition. Cohen defines scarcity thus:

> Here is what we understand by scarcity: given men's wants and the character of external nature, they cannot satisfy their wants unless they spend the better part of their time and energy doing what they would rather not do, engaged in labour which is not experienced as an end in itself. (p. 152)

Cohen assumes that the historical situation is one of scarcity. This would appear to be a commonplace; surely the primitive condition of mankind was one in which he was driven by objective necessity to struggle unceasingly to find the necessaries of life. The anthropologist Marshall Sahlins, in his paper 'The Original Affluent Society' in *Stone Age Economics*, confronts this thesis head on. He argues that this is a presumption on the part of Western observers, themselves unable to survive in such environments as the Australian deserts, and who are frequently falsified by their own ethnographic accounts. He argues that scarcity is not the lot of many 'primitive' peoples, showing how they obtain the means of livelihood customary to them with modest amounts of labour and adequate time for leisure and cultural activities. Their route to want satisfaction lies in the cultural limitation of wants to such as match the means available to attain them. Need alone will not provide the motive force for development out of the hunting and gathering stage. In like manner the economist Amartya Sen in *Poverty and Famines* shows that famines in the twentieth century are seldom the result of a simple shortfall of food, but are the products of distributive patterns. Scarcity is a category that invites investigation and cannot be presumed as a self-evident proposition.

For Cohen the level of development of the forces of production must be specified in order to prove that they have progressed through time. His criterion is as follows:

> the development of the productive forces may be identified with the growth in the surplus they make possible and this in turn may be identified with the amount of the day which remains after the labouring time required to maintain the producers has been subtracted. (p. 61)

Alex Callinicos (*Is there a Future for Marxism?*, p. 145) pertinently points out that this is in no sense independent of the relations of production. Heightened exploitation through relative surplus value, is compatible, indeed directly connected, with a shorter working day. The intensity of labour is directly connected to the relations of production. Moreover, given Cohen's definition, hunters and gatherers really do form the 'original affluent society'. If the labour time involved in providing the means of subsistence for everybody is short, say six hours, and less than the industrial working day, then what distinguishes the development of the productive forces in capitalism from hunting and gathering societies? To be sure this latter's surplus consists in leisure time rather than 'material' products, but is this not Cohen's ideal? It would seem that the 'intelligence of a kind and degree' which Cohen deems men to possess would lead them to conclude that they could not 'improve' their situation.

As to the first proposition Cohen says men are 'somewhat rational'. In one sense it is difficult to disagree with this proposition, to assert that men are systematically irrational would be absurd. The real problem is to specify in what 'rationality' might consist. Rationality for Cohen does not consist in intelligence since this is the subject of a separate proposition and is not peculiar to men; other mammals Cohen recognises are able to modify their behaviour through learning to change their situation. Rationality consists in perceiving that a state of affairs is in one's interest and doing what is necessary to bring it about. Cohen explains this later on as follows: 'But why should the fact that the relations restrict the forces foretell their doom, if not because it is irrational to persist with them given the price in lost opportunity of further inroads against scarcity?' (p. 159) The forces of production develop in the direction of the diminution of scarcity. Now Cohen supposes that men have an 'interest' in reducing scarcity and this can only be a 'material' interest and not a 'social one' tied to the relations of production. We have noted the difficulty of separating the material from the welter of beliefs and activities which are part and parcel of society, including its production and distribution. A material interest must be expressed independently of ideologies and beliefs which support the relations of production. It is difficult to determine the forms of rationality which might support such a material interest other than in supposing direct producers have a material hedonistic outlook, a secular commitment to increasing productivity. But even if the direct producers *did* have such an outlook they have seldom been of much account against those who own the means of production. Further, suppose the direct producers are imbued with a Buddhist ethic or are sincere Christians oriented to the afterlife and a belief in the virtues of poverty. For them to extend the forces of production, to invest time and energy in such a secular objective, is *irrational* according to their scheme of beliefs and the interests which follow from them. Cohen does not demonstrate that large groups of men for large periods of time have had the interest he ascribes to them – indeed, he spends a great deal of time juggling with the well-known fact that many pre-capitalist societies have not evidenced the healthy attention to develop productivity which ought to follow if the rationality he attributes to men in general were really such a powerful interest.

Cohen ultimately grounds his thesis on the commonsense assumption that the forces of production *have* developed through history, and that less productive forces seldom succeed more productive ones. Now most people would accept this proposition as intuitively true, even if they are aware of the difficulties of measuring output and productivity within, let alone between, systems of production. However, this will not help Cohen since such an intuitively 'obvious fact' is capable of many explanations; in particular it is explicable by the role of the relations of production. It would not have satisfied Marx, since for him the development of the forces of production is a necessary tendency and not a mere generalisation or happenstance.

Even if we assume rationality means what Cohen says it does and that men do indeed have such a perceived interest does this lead to the development of the forces of production? Cohen's claim is that men have an interest in reducing 'scarcity'. Now he defines the 'surplus' as being 'identified' with the 'amount of the day which remains after the labouring time required to maintain the producers has been subtracted'. There is an ambiguity here since 'surplus' on this definition, as we have seen, might mean a quantum of leisure time. Let us suppose for the moment that reducing scarcity means increasing the quantities of products available to society, some of which rub off on their producers. What this proves, if we accept Cohen's terms of argument, is that the producers have an interest in greater *output* and not necessarily in developing the 'forces of production'. The two are not the same. Greater output meets this interest in reducing scarcity immediately, assuming it to be possible with definite and limited additions to, or more efficient utilisation of, the factors of production. And most systems of production most of the time operate well below capacity. The official histories of war production for the UK and the USA in the Second World War bear this out dramatically. Many systems of production can make substantial inroads into 'scarcity' (accepting Cohen's account of it) by doing what they do better or at a slightly greater intensity of labour. The benefits are immediate. The development of the forces of production, however, does not promise such immediate benefits. It may involve prolonged investment in perfecting new processes and ways of working, 'research and development' in modern parlance, even if the 'forces' in question be the perfection of firing pottery or the formation of the factory system. In the short run the necessary investment of means of production and labour may cause output to *decline* relative to the most efficient utilisation of existing systems. Considered in the light of Cohen's account of rationality, the assessment of whether such development is 'worth' it must come down to an assumption of compensating long-run returns. This is a form of economic calculation which could go one way or the other on Cohen's premises. The development of the forces of production might be rationally rejected in favour of short-run considerations of output.

Cohen ignores the nature of the calculating agency. He is able to do so by the opposition material/social and by the supposition of a 'pure' subject with a direct material interest. But economic agents are not of this kind, they do have definite means of calculation connected with the relations of production and they are not 'material' entities, but agents with a social position. The problem is not one of irrationality but of competing economic rationali*ties*. There is no 'reason' *tout court*, rather there are definite forms of economic calculation and also definite non-economic schemes for patterning conduct which are economically consequential. These show the distinctive influence of the relations of production.

Take A. V. Chayanov's theory of peasant economic calculation. Chayanov posits a form of marginalist calculation by the peasant enterprise, the family labour farm, in which an equilibrium between labour effort and consumption is established. Accept this theory and it follows that *output* stagnates well below its theoretical limits, the enterprise members trading off the satisfactions of increased output against the marginal disutility of additional labour. Here we see a form of calculation which not merely limits output but systematically discriminates against the investments necessary to develop the forces of production. It meets Cohen's criteria of rationality since it addresses itself to the merits of additional output, and it finds them wanting, because involving additional effort. Another example of such a response would be the pattern of economic action underlying Mark Elvin's 'high level equilibrium trap' in *The Pattern of the Chinese Past* in which Chinese agriculture becomes locked in to a regime of high yields per acre at the cost of equally high labour inputs, a product of a pattern of seeking immediate increases in output by additional efforts within an existing system of production. Such a system once established discriminates against innovation because of the massive efforts required to maintain existing inputs and patterns of working. Such a system is not irrational if inflexible; it comes about through a preference for accretions to output – in themselves rational – and which would involve unacceptable costs in any given period to unscramble. In both examples we can reconstruct a rational case *against* development of the forces of production, knowing as we do the characteristics of the enterprises and calculating agents enmeshed in definite relations of production. Both accounts have their defects, but this does not alter the fact that there is no account of the forms of calculating agents or the methods of calculation in Cohen's account of the primacy thesis. Even if we accept many of his terms of argument he is unable to show *how* 'rationality' leads to the development of the forces of production, and this is inevitable given his abstraction of rationality from economic agents enmeshed in definite relations of production. His separation of the material and social domains of social life may be necessary to the formulation of his thesis of primacy, but this abstraction of economic agents from their social context has as its consequences a fatal inability to deal with how economic actors act.

Cohen's attempt to 'defend' Marx's theory of history is on balance a failure, although forcefully and clearly argued. It abstracts from the complex and contradictory combination which is Marx's discourse: even if it were vindicated its title would have to be '*Part* of Karl Marx's Theory of History: A Defence'. It fails to establish its claim to demonstrate the primacy of the 'forces of production', although it has the merit of bringing the deficencies glaringly to light. It fails, but it does so not in pursuing some eccentricity of Cohen's but a central proposition in Marxist discourse.

Chapter 3

Collingwood, Relativism and the Purposes of History

E. H. Carr contended that R. G. Collingwood was 'the only British thinker in the present century who has made a serious contribution to the philosophy of history' (*What is History?*, p. 21). We should be clear here to what form of philosophy of history Collingwood made a contribution. Certainly not to the philosophy of history in the sense of an explanatory scheme which seeks to rationalise the whole of history as a necessary story. Rather, Collingwood was concerned to account for the practice of historical writing, to theorise the activity of historians. For him history is a distinct field of investigation with its own object and methods. In *The Idea of History*, he produced a fundamental critique of positivist conceptions of historiography and a defence of history as an 'autonomous' science. History as a fully autonomous domain of investigation is a relatively recent development, long pre-dated by other practices of historical writing which he calls 'scissors and paste' history.

We shall see that Carr's judgment is correct but that his account of Collingwood is less than accurate. Collingwood is certainly concerned to challenge the positivist conception of the historian's object, but this does not lead to the consequences Carr attributes to Collingwood's doctrine. In the positivist position which Collingwood challenges the object of history consists essentially in a set of given 'facts' about the past. The past is a spectacle, a procession of events which passes as if in review before the historian. This past Collingwood terms a 'dead' past, it is a fixed and unalterable collection of data. The historian is an archivist, who tells the story given to him through records of past events. The ideal of positivist historiography is summed up by Ranke's claim that the task of the historian is 'simply to show how it really was'.

But what 'was' it we are enjoined to show the 'how' of? The

positivist conception of the past as innumerable given facts disperses the consistency of the object of history. To which 'facts', to which events do we give attention? We know that recorded facts are only a sample of past events. We know that Julius Caesar crossed the Rubicon, but so have thousands of others and we do not consider them to be objects of historical knowledge. If positivism's claims were true it would be immobilised before the vast mass of recorded facts and helpless to recover the even larger number of facts which have gone unrecorded. Positivism's ideal is a 'scissors and paste' history, helpless before its archive and condemned to repeat it. It cannot ask independent questions of this given mass of data, it cannot alter it according to the operations of knowledge but is condemned merely to arrange it.

Of what possible relevance can this study of a 'dead' past be? Even if positivism's ideal were possible, if innumerable facts could be put in objective order without the active intervention of the operations of knowledge, what would this tell us? That certain things happened and are no more. For Collingwood, historical writing can only have contemporary relevance if its object is not a dead but a 'living' past, if the historian is in no way separated from his object. The 'past', our records, once existed as a present, actively shaped both as records and events by human actors, and it is re-constructed in a present. Historical 'facts' are not given but constructed. Testimony, documents, etc., record the significances of the dead who were once contemporaries. We select from these products of a selective process, testimony, documents, etc., on the basis of our judgments of veracity and significance. This is as true of the working historian who spurns 'explanations' as it is of the historical investigator who asks definite questions and seeks answers in historical materials. Positivism tries to establish an impossible practice, its objectivity is immobilised by the mass of supposed 'data' it must selectively order to tell its stories. The process of selection characteristic of *all* historical writing is governed by considerations of contemporary relevance, and its selectivity changes with contemporary concerns. Hence all historical writing is about the 'present'. Collingwood says:

> St. Augustine looked at history from the point of view of the early Christian. . . . Gibbon from that of an eighteenth century Englishman; Mommsen from that of a nineteenth century

German. There is no point in asking which was the right point of view. Each was only possible for the man who adopted it. (*Idea*, p. xii)

Carr contends that this leads to a wilful relativism – a 'total scepticism' (*What is History?*, p. 20). Collingwood's rejection of positivism leads him near to the opposite error of idealism: 'Collingwood, in his reaction against "scissors-and-paste history", against the view of history as a mere compilation of facts, comes perilously near to treating history as something spun out of the human brain.' (*ibid.*)

This view of history as 'an infinity of meanings' tends to a pragmatist conception of knowledge, in 'that the criterion of a right interpretation is its suitability for some present purpose'. (p. 27) Collingwood is apparently a hairsbreadth away from Nietzschean irrationalism. Carr's view of Collingwood is widespread. He is frequently regarded as an 'idealist', either an English disciple of Croce or the last link in the chain of English neo-Hegelian idealism, and an incurable relativist. He is neither. Collingwood is concerned to secure historical knowledge against relativism and to defend not merely the relevance but the moral value of historical knowledge. Collingwood became a militant anti-Nazi and was utterly opposed to the use of history for irrationalist myth-making. Collingwood sought a conception of truth which indeed could not be outside its time, but which would be as right as it was possible to be *in* its time, which was not true because separated from presuppositions, questions and value positions, but true *because* of them.

Collingwood was well aware of the conclusion Carr would later attempt to draw from his work and rebuts it. His object is not to create a relativising historicism, but to find a way out of it. The purpose of situating past historical knowledges in terms of the questions asked by historians, to see their histories as distinct answers stemming from definite presuppositions, is not to make them all equal. It is to differentiate them in terms of their value as knowledge by discovering what these questions, presuppositions and answers were. Herodotus is not at par with other Greeks who regard the world of events as a mere screen of shifting and changing appearances. Herodotus and Thucydides stand out by not subscribing to the presupposition dominant in Greek philosophy that valid knowledge is of what is unchanging and eternal. Collingwood reconstructs historiography by asking – to what questions were historians' forms of writing and investigation answers? He ranks historians' contributions by the character of the questions they asked; it is this which governs the productivity of their answers. Were Collingwood as systematic a relativist as Carr makes out there could be no grounds for contrasting 'scissors-and-paste' history with an autonomous investigative historiography; each would be appropriate to its chosen purposes.

Collingwood, on the contrary, wants to show why positivism is condemned to the celebration of 'scissors-and-paste' history, and in consequence both to an impossible project and to a pernicious species of relativism. To assess historical events from the standpoint of their contemporary significance is the only way that relativistic historicism can be avoided, in which we can by answering our own questions in terms of the historical record give answers whose value is not merely relative to past events.

A positivist history is, in fact, relativistic since it claims all 'facts' are at par with one another and given in their significance in their own time and no other. If positivism's ideal is as Ranke claims it to be, if it purports only to establish 'how it really was' then it cannot explain *why* it was this and not that. A positivist history is both given and contingent, but that contingency is beyond question in positivism's acceptance of its object as given. It must take what is given to it and accept it as such.

A positivist conception of the object of history as a 'dead' past is moreover compatible with a natural scientific conception of explanation. If history, the account of past human actions, is accommodated to explanation in terms of cause and effect then this too leads to a species of relativism. Such a conception of explanation is reductionist, it converts actions into the effects of causes. In ignoring the specific origins of human actions in meanings and intentions it makes the source of events extrinsic to human purposes, reduces all actions having the same causes to events of the same class and denies them differential significance. Actions are relative to causes, and derive their significance from the relative importance of their causes in the scheme of things. This means that all effects of the same class, having one origin in a common type of cause, are the same. Thus, there can be no 'autonomous' histories of philosophy, or the arts, that is, of those activities viewed as continuous enterprises attempting to fulfil certain purposes, the products of these activities having differential significance in so far as they approach to attaining these purposes. Such domains are the effects of external causes and at each period are no more than the traces of these causes. Thus Collingwood regards Marx as an economic reductionist, treating forms of social consciousness as the reflections of the real material relations of society. The very conception of an 'autonomous' history of philosophy, for example, is here treated as an illusion; rather we see a series of effects reducible to causes acting at a particular time. The result is an historicism, products of human 'objective mind' are treated as no more than reflections of their time. Hegel betrayed his profound understanding that history is the history of thought – not a causal natural science – and that it explains affairs as the working of 'reason'. He did so in his *Philosophy of History* by giving the dynamic role to the nation and the state and treating consciousness as the medium of reflection of the distinct national 'spirits'. For Collingwood the Hegel to be emulated is the author of the *Lectures on the History of Philosophy*, who treats philosophy as an enterprise of autonomous mind developing by solving its own problems. Whether Collingwood's account of either Marx or Hegel is an accurate one is not at issue here. His point is that all history is properly the history of *thought*, that it cannot be explained causally without being treated reductively. Collingwood's view is not without its problems, as we shall see, but it does mount a powerful critique of the reductionism inherent in attempts to reduce history to an objective causal scheme. What is significant in such a scheme are not products, like works of art, but the causes which underlie them. Significance consists in relative causal weight and its hierarchy is a hierarchy of *causes*. Such significance is condemned to exist only in its own time, if the causes are confined to a definite period, or outside of time, if the causes act with the same relative weight and effect throughout history. In consequence we cannot make historical judgments of the relative merit, value or significance of the products of human action. Events are confined to their time and the causes acting on them. Once such causes cease to act those events become part of a 'dead' past and if these causes act today then history is not a distinctive knowledge, but the store of examples for a contemporary causal sociology.

Collingwood thus argues for the separation of the historical or cultural sciences and the natural sciences. He repeats a division in knowledge propounded by German neo-Kantians like Dilthey and by Croce. History cannot be comprehended as a practice if it is modelled on the natural sciences' search for general laws; rather it is an individualising science which understands and therefore explains past human action in its own special way.

History can only be *human* history. Sciences like geology which reconstruct sequences of events are not history. For the past they reconstruct is a dead past without contemporary human significance. Collingwood says:

> The processes of nature can therefore be properly described as sequences of mere events, but those of history cannot. They are not processes of mere events but processes of actions, which have an inner side, consisting of processes of thought and what the historian is looking for is those processes of thought. All history is the history of thought. (*Idea*, p. 215)

This may appear idealist but it is not meant to be so. Thought is neither subjective consciousness nor mere experience. The thought Collingwood is concerned with is what Hegel called 'objective mind'; it identifies itself in its products and objectifies itself as those products. 'The historical process is itself a process of thought' (p. 226) and 'Of everything other than thought there can be no history.' (p. 304) For Collingwood there cannot be actions without thought, for it is thought which constructs the situation in such a way that an action of a certain type becomes possible and necessary. Events are the outcomes of actions and thought is necessary for actions to be constructed; they are prefigured as events in thought. Therefore, to explain historical action is to *understand* the thoughts which led to actions. History is a province of objectified mind and nothing else, for unless events are intelligible, conceivable as prefigured in thought then they have no meaning. It is only the reconstruction of the thoughts of actors, in so far as they construct situations of action, that enables us to describe past events. And it is only the possession of accounts of actions which enables us to do this. History without means of access to thought is impossible. It is only the availability of objectified mind which enables us to reconstruct what past actions *were* and to measure their consequences by their prefiguration in mind. Mind for Collingwood is not 'consciousness' but is at one with its products and the processes of reflections which produce them.

It is not only history as a discipline which reconstructs past processes of thought; all thought is historical. The historian's processes of understanding are not different in kind from the systematic reconstruction and review of our own past thoughts and actions which we use to develop our knowledge and in practical affairs.

It is only by historical thinking that I can discover what I thought ten years ago, by reading what I then wrote, or what I thought five minutes ago, by reflecting on an action that I then did, which surprised me when I realised what I had done. In this sense all knowledge of mind is historical. (p. 219)

This is why the past is a 'living past', as thought objectified in its products it can be reviewed in thought. To the extent that we can re-activate it, re-think it, it is both intelligible and capable of current relevance. Without this capacity it becomes dead and unintelligble. In Collingwood's example in the *Autobiography* charters in Medieval Latin can be read and interpreted because a knowledge of Latin remains a living resource of contemporary thought, whereas at the time he was writing documents written in Linear B could not because there were no means to read them. We could infer that the people of Minoan Crete could write but little else.

Collingwood is committed to a view of history as the history of thought because it is the product of definite individual human actors. Nations, states, classes, etc., are merely hypostatisations of related individual human actions. Nations exist only in so far as individual actors think in terms of nations, construct their situations of action in terms of them and act accordingly. Such things are not entities but categories of thought, forms of belief active in the thought-processes of actors. Hence history can only be concerned with 'actors' and with situations of action as the thoughts of actors. Situations do not exist except as patterns of thought:

All history is the history of thought; and when an historian says that a man is in a certain situation this is the same as saying that he thinks he is in this situation. The hard facts of the situation, which it is so important for him to face, are the hard facts of the way in which he conceives the situation. (*Idea*, p. 317)

What men believe is consequential and is not affected by our views as to the justifiability of that belief. If a man acts out of belief in the existence of devils (*Idea*, p. 317) we cannot dismiss his action because we believe such notions to be the products of mere superstition: 'wrong ways of thinking are just as much historical facts as right ones, and, no less than they, determine the situation (always a thought situation) in which the man who shares them is placed.' (*Idea*, p. 317) Men are free in that their thought is not the product of causes, whether natural or psychological. They are free both when we consider their thoughts justified and when we do not. Collingwood claims: 'Historical thought, thought about rational activity, is free from the domination of natural science, and rational activity is free from the domination of nature.' (p. 318) This freedom does not consist in being right; rational activity includes 'superstition' for rational here means the product of reasoning and says nothing about the quality of that reasoning. Reason is an independent activity of mind, not a psychological thought-process occasioned by any cause. Mind is a distinct realm, it is thought's autonomous action embodied in definite products.

This status of thought and mind explains how the thoughts of historical actors are to be approached. Again it is an error to convert mind into nature – into a psychology. Hence Collingwood rejects the evolutionism of a Herbert Spencer or the cyclicism of an Oswald Spengler. In such systems mind becomes the effect of a supra-mental process; it is conditioned by causes acting at a definite time to produce 'thoughts' of a certain character and these thoughts are subsequently superseded and replaced by others which are the result of causes acting in changed conditions. The result is a radical relativism:

The past, in a natural process, is a past superseded or dead. Now suppose the historical process of human thought were in this sense an evolutionary process. It would follow that the ways of thinking characteristic of any given historical period are the ways in which people must think then, but in which others, cast in different times in a different mental mould, cannot think at all. If that were the case, there would be no such thing as truth. (*Idea*, p. 225)

Evolution is only conceivable as a natural process and as one which cannot serve as a resource for contemporary human action: 'The Trilobites of the Silurian age may be the ancestors of the mammals today, including ourselves; but a human being is not a kind of wood louse.' (*Ibid.*)

The adequacy of Collingwood's views of the value of palaeontology or the theory of natural selection are not at issue here. Although it must be said that a knowledge of human evolution and a recognition that humans have been shaped in their capacities by natural selection is neither 'dead' nor of no contemporary relevance. It would clearly be of value to Collingwood's history of 'thought' to know how and why homo sapiens acquired the capacity to produce Collingwood's products of objective mind. Collingwood's point, however, is that such products of mind can always be re-activated and continued in the present. Julius Caesar may be dead but his actions are neither dead nor irrelevant – they exist contemporaneously in the claims and re-enactments of Mussolini. Spinoza's thought is not 'past' but a contemporary resource of philosophical argument and commentary. It can be of value in teaching, for example. The human 'past' is thus contemporary and living.

For Collingwood the reconstruction of the past in terms of contemporary significance is neither relativist nor idealist – its value depends on what we do with it in the present. It is only in its contemporary use that history can have a non-historicist and non-relativist status, a lasting value beyond given dead events and a significance for us beyond that of being the equivalent effects of causes of a particular type.

Truth is itself historical. All truth is only available to us by the method of question and answer, problematising our questions by the quality of the answers we receive. To recognise this historicity is not to historicise truth, to make knowledge no more than the expression of its own time. Knowledge develops by working over the past products of its activity, by asking new questions on the basis of criticism of old answers and marshalling new evidence relevant to those questions. Collingwood asks: 'How can we ever satisfy ourselves that the principles on which we think are true, except by going on thinking according to those principles, and seeing whether unanswerable criticisms of them emerge as we work?' (*Idea*, p. 230). Collingwood is not an epistemological

thinker in the sense of seeking to find a mechanism whereby
knowledge can be grounded, that we can be assured that
knowledge does produce a correspondence between its explanations and reality. We cannot satisfy ourselves that what we know
is true by founding or guaranteeing the processes of our knowledge,
we can only use those processes to answer definite questions. In
modern terms Collingwood is saying truth is relative to a
'conceptual scheme', evidentiality is governed by the questions we
ask. And as in Lakatos's methodology of scientific research
programmes, knowledge is assessed by the productivity of the
questions it asks.

The questions history asks are about the thought of past actors.
How does the historian reconstruct the thought of such actors?
Collingwood's answer is deceptively simple: by making that
thought one's own. In this Collingwood appears to follow Dilthey
and Croce. He differs from Dilthey, he claims, in not reducing such
re-enactment to psychology. Such a reduction will result either in a
species of naturalism or in an attempt to re-create the subjective
experience of a consciousness in all its immediacy, in Hegel's terms
to engage in 'subjective idealism'. The object is not to enter into the
experience of the subject but to comprehend objective mind, to
understand thoughts which are not simply subjective. The account
of the thought in question must be sustained by constructing
evidence as to what it is and by isolating its specificity by posing
questions relevant to its context. Such reconstruction is neither
emotive sympathy nor wilful play-acting. The object is not to 'be'
Caesar or Nelson, qua individual, but to reconstruct the actor qua
actor and his situation. It is to raise questions about the possibility
and consistency of accounts of actions, and is subject to the
demands of truth – such reconstruction must be subject to tests and
provide evidence. This is not possible if the exercise is the re-
creation of another mind as its own subjective experience.
Collingwood insists that: 'The historian cannot apprehend the
individual act of thought in its individuality, just as it actually
happened!' (*Idea*, p. 303). The historian's aim is to gain access to

the way in which thought, transcending its own immediacy,
survives and revives in other contexts: and to express the truth
that individual acts and persons appear in history not in virtue of
their individuality as such, but because that individuality is the

vehicle of a thought which, because it was actually theirs is, potentially, everyone's. (*ibid.*)

History, however, is more than 'scissors and paste', the mere dependence on what testimony and authorities say. Such testimony and authorities must be questioned. Historical reasoning involves inferences about actions, and these are more than suppositions based on induction from the 'facts'. Inferences enable us to question facts and seek new evidence, because they aim to establish the *necessity* of a given course of action. Collingwood argues that inferential reasoning enables us to establish why something was so and could not be otherwise. Whilst history is not a natural science of generalising laws, and its objects thereby necessary because they are cases of the action of such laws, its conclusions about the actions and thoughts which form its objects are no less rigorous. It is a science of concrete instances of human action and thought which explains why they were so.

In contrasting 'scientific history' with scissors and paste history, Collingwood argues that the historian has independent means of knowledge which are not helpless before the authorities. He adopts Francis Bacon's metaphor that the natural philosopher, in order to produce useful knowledge, must 'put nature to the question'. He is clear what the phrase means, for to be 'put to the question' in the seventeenth century meant judicial investigation under torture. What instruments does the historian possess? Collingwood says: 'history finds its proper method when the historian puts his authorities in the witness-box, and by cross-questioning extorts from them information which in their original statements they have withheld.' (*Idea*, p. 237) If history for Collingwood is the history of thought, it is not confined in its methods either to documents or to merely asking questions of documents. In his *Autobiography* Collingwood makes it clear that archaeology provides the historian with an experimental means of questioning and supplementing history as present in written records. Other resources are available such as numismatics, palaeography, philology, the statistical analysis of records and so on. All these provide resources of evidence which enable us to answer questions. Collingwood, far from being an idealist empathiser with other minds, would not spurn the 'new archaeology' or 'quantitative history'. He would regard them as valuable means to ask new questions. These questions, however, are about how and why men acted as they did. To take another example, a work like Fernand Braudel's *The Mediterranean and the Mediterranean World in the Age of Philip II* might appear the antithesis of Collingwood's conception of the historian's practice on a superficial reading. But such a work which stresses the geographical and social environment of historical action is in no sense antagonistic to Collingwood's conception of history as the history of thought. He could regard it as providing powerful evidence of the context of thought and action. The relative historical continuity of the technical and environmental situation between the late Middle Ages and the eighteenth century in no way undercuts Collingwood's position, any more than would the transformations in chronology produced by radio-carbon 14 dating.

Collingwood's conception of the nature of historical evidence is open-ended:

> Everything is evidence which the historian can use as evidence. But what can he so use? It must be something here and now perceptible to him: this written page, the spoken utterance, this building, this finger print. And of all the things perceptible to him there is not one which he might not conceivably use as evidence on some question, if he came to it with the right question in mind. The enlargement of historical knowledge comes about mainly through finding how to use as evidence this or that kind of perceived fact which historians have hitherto thought useless to them. (*Idea*, p. 247)

To realise that what is evidential changes with the nature of our questions and is valid as evidence only in relation to them 'is not an argument for historical scepticism' (*Idea*, p. 248). It does mean that 'every new generation must rewrite history in its own way'. (*ibid.*) This does not invalidate or undermine historical work, rather it increases the scope of questions and materials available to historians to activate in some future present. Historical knowledge works by posing, re-posing and displacing questions, *not* by accumulating 'evidence' independently of them. Facts are not given, it is only relative to a question that we can begin to assess the value of those materials which are to constitute evidence for the answer to it: 'Question and evidence, in history, are correlative. Anything is evidence which enables you to answer your question.' (*Idea*, p. 281)

To say that history is concerned with thought is not to confine its materials to 'ideas', far from it. Anything which enables us to understand mind in its context can be used. 'Mind' is not a category confined to consciousness, it is the active substance of social being and the central component in social relations. Actors do not exist out of a context but that context is what it is by the way it is apprehended in knowledge and belief.

Collingwood is often portrayed as the final fling of the decaying tradition of English idealism. A woolly thinker committed to speculative re-enactment of the subjective states of past actors. A close reading of *The Idea of History* and the *Autobiography* will show not merely that he forestalled these objections but that he produced powerful arguments to show the relativism implicit in positivism and naturalism in historical method.

It should not be imagined that Collingwood's theory of history is one I subscribe to. It clearly would be of some service to Edward Thompson to give clarity and force to his idea of history as the contestation of values. Although he would find its conception of historical evidence, that facts are not given, less than congenial and its commitment to a species of methodological individualism problematic. This latter commitment is a central component of Collingwood's doctrine, as is the related and consequential rationalist account of objective mind. Powerful arguments can be mounted against both – Collingwood subscribes to a variant of what Barry Hindess has characterised as the 'rationalist conception of action' (*Sociological Theories of the Economy*, Ch. 6). Collingwood's account of Freud (*Autobiography*, p. 95) is inadequate in the extreme, although it pays him due respect, and one would expect this from a theory which sees the significant aspect of concrete actors' motivations as consisting in elaborated intentions and purposes. To insist that psychology can only lead to a naturalistic and reductive account of human action is to misconceive both that action and the possible forms of non-reductive explanation in psychology. Collingwood's rigid separation of the historical and natural sciences, one which does not disparage natural science although it misconceives it as exclusively identified with the search for general natural laws, retains many of the defects of the *Geisteswissenschaft* tradition. Collingwood cannot see the value of evolutionary biology in the analysis of human affairs. It must rigidly separate man-as-actor from man-as-animal, a funda-

mental defect when we try to explain the development of humans'
capacities for social relations. To list one's criticisms of Collingwood would, however, distract us from our purpose, to encourage
Marxists to read him. Collingwood's account of knowledge as a
process of question and answer has much to recommend it; its
value goes beyond historical knowledge. So, too, does Collingwood's insistence that historical writing must find its point of
departure in the questions we must ask ourselves in the present, and
to which historical materials form part of the answer. Collingwood
sets himself against the twin historiographical vices of archivism
and the production of meta-historical explanatory schemes. Both
are problematic because they legitimate the conception of the whole
past as the available domain of the historian, as conceptions of
inquiry they divert us from current concerns. Collingwood asks of
the historian that he or she seek in historical materials answers to
current problems. He is the philosopher of history as a strategy for
asking questions about ourselves, not as the celebration of the past
as an archive to be endlessly explored.

Chapter 4

The Necessity of Theory –
A Critique of E. P. Thompson's
The Poverty of Theory *

Edward Thompson considers his essay *The Poverty of Theory* a declaration of war between theology and reason.[1] Althusser's work represents the highest stage of Stalinism: 'it is a straightforward ideological police action' (p. 275). It is an enemy to the left which must be 'exposed' and 'driven out'. The depth of Thompson's hatred of Althusserianism can be gauged from his confession: 'If I thought that Althusserianism was the logical terminus of Marxist thought, then I could never be a Marxist. I would rather be a Christian.' (p. 381) Fortunately for him he is spared the spurious choice. Althusserianism is merely one of a number of dogmatic Marx*isms* which betray Marx's true legacy of 'active reason'.[2]

There will always be 'enemies to the left', socialist theories and political doctrines which can find no common ground. Sometimes their struggle takes a tragic form, of armed struggle and the liquidation of opponents by the state. In the case of Thompson's war the struggle is tragi-comic in its weapons and objectives. Thompson strikes out at his enemies – with ridicule, some of which is funny, some so ignorant and unjust as to demean its author; with the passionate expression of values, some of which one hopes all socialists share, others of which reveal his refusal to leave the nineteenth century; and with arguments, some of which although accurate criticisms are several years too late to be original and have been better made by the despised 'Althusserians' themselves, others of which reveal an elementary incomprehension of Althusser's work. Some of Thompson's objectives have a certain validity. He is

* First published in *Economy and Society*, Vol. 8, No. 4, November 1979.

not alone in fearing the consequences of the encapsulation of the Marxist intelligentsia in an infinite meta-critical discourse on Marxism itself. This is equally the concern of some of his despised 'Althusserian' opponents, although he cannot see this through blind passion. Others of his objectives have everything in common with the practices of the Stalinism he so rightly loathes. When it comes to Althusserians he wants to shut their mouths, albeit with words, but words wielded as recklessly as a club.

I have no intention of using words as a club to strike back. The Left is too weak and aimless in this country to afford to let itself be further divided by struggles it can avoid. This is not to overrate the importance either of Edward Thompson or British Althusserianism, the world can get along without us. It is, rather, to recognise that these differences are symptomatic of a wider and destructive mode of controversy which isolates and divides the Left intelligentsia. I do not regard Thompson as an enemy who must be driven out and shut up. I value and respect his polemics in defence of civil liberties. But I do not agree with his conception of socialist politics or the type of intellectual work which should support it. It is an urgent necessity that socialists find means to *differ* which do not destroy the wider possibilities of communication. What is absurd is to differ in such a way that neither side *learns* anything, and least of all about the other.

Louis Althusser can defend himself. His works, those of Poulantzas, Barry Hindess and myself are there to be read – repeating them will not silence Thompson's distortions. Instead, I intend to examine what Edward Thompson offers us as an alternative practice of Marxism to its hated caricature in the form of Althusserianism. On the one hand, I will show that his alternative is no less radical a renunciation of the dubious heritage of Marxist 'orthodoxy' than is Althusser's or our own. Thompson is no saviour of Marxism, except in the sense of the surgeon who to save a man's life amputates above the neck. On the other hand, I will contend that what Thompson offers removes one essential part of that heritage which is indispensable, the conception of Marxist theory as a strategic guide to political practice, and this at a time when the radical re-thinking and re-direction of that practice was never more necessary if we are to have an effective democratic socialist movement in this country.

But before I do so I must finish with the manner of Thompson's critique. Thompson employs imagery so frequently and thought-lessly that parts of his text have an oneiric quality, they amount to a presentation of its unconscious. This imagery, although vivid, is often destructive, and yet revealing:

> A cloud no bigger than a man's hand crosses the English Channel from Paris, and then, in an instant, the trees, the orchard, the hedgerows, the field of wheat, are black with locusts. When at length they rise to fly on to the next parish, the boughs are bared of all culture, the fields have been stripped of every green blade of human aspiration: and in those skeletal forms and that blackened landscape, theoretical practice announces its 'discovery': the mode of production. (pp. 358–9)*

Thus Thompson the squire of Empirica Parva (p. 188) beset by a foreign pestilence, alien in essence to British life. Thompson assures us he has great respect for the right kind of French intellectuals (*Annales*, and Pierre Bourdieu, for example). But this is the metaphorics of xenophobia – and there are numerous other instances. What Thompson reveals here is the depth of his belief that there is a characteristic British tradition and culture. I think this notion of a fundamental national culture orientation is a myth. It sustains in Thompson's case a conception that British socialism needs a re-statement of its fundamental and ever-present values. In pursuit of this myth Marx is to be made compatible with the epistemological prejudices legitimised as the 'British empirical tradition'. The need for radical re-thinking of the nature of socialist social relations as an objective of socialist political practice and of the forms of that practice itself are thereby denied and rendered unposable as a problem. What we need is a re-vitalisation and awakening of the living traditions of the English working class, blighted in their expression by Stalinism and social democracy.

If only Thompson's phantom armies awaited his call:

> In Britain, with its small and declining Communist Party, these questions are of secondary importance. But, equally, the failure of the alternative libertarian tradition, to enter the vacuum and establish itself as a political presence alongside the labour movement – this failure is the more serious and less explicable. (p. 383)

*All references are to *The Poverty of Theory* unless otherwise stated.

Indeed, *inexplicable* if there is this vital class culture and a vital libertarian intellectual tradition stemming back to Blake and beyond. Thompson refuses to recognise his failure – not his alone but the common failure of the democratic socialist Left – even as he speaks it.

Thompson has relegated Althusserianism to the brains of foreign locusts. At the same time he finds its influence prevalent in British higher education. He copes with this paradox by reducing the victims of this noxious influence to para-intellectuals ignorant of real culture. Only such people could ever welcome the 'freak' that is Althusserianism:

> They might be right in their first assumption – that Althusserian 'Marxism' is an intellectual freak – but it will not for that reason go away. Historians should know that freaks if tolerated – and even if fattened and fed – can show astonishing influence and longevity (after all to the rational mind, the greater part of the history of ideas is the history of freaks). This particular freak . . . has now lodged itself firmly in a particular social *couche*, the *bourgeois lumpen-intelligentsia*: aspirant intellectuals, whose amateurish intellectual preparation disarms them before manifest absurdities and elementary philosophical blunders, and whose innocence in intellectual *practice* leaves them paralysed in the first web of scholastic argument they encounter (and so on, p. 195)

What is shocking about this passage is the juncture it effects between two reactionary and obscurantist modes of discourse: the Marxist invalidation of ideas by reference to their social origin, and the distaste for novelty in the established official intellectual seeking to impose what he thinks a fit apprenticeship on new members of the club. Thompson can regard – if we let his imagery *argue* for him – as wholly negative the breakdown of the established relations of hierarchy, apprenticeship and clientship, and the introduction of new subjects like sociology, which resulted from the unprecedented expansion of higher education since the war. In breaking down the established academic 'police' mechanisms this expansion created the conditions for innovation and free debate. Some of the products of this new openness may be ephemeral and extreme, but its general effect has been liberating and positive. It has created the conditions for a Marxist intelligentsia on a mass scale. Thompson is no simple academic snob, he showed his contempt for such considerations by giving up his chair. But his imagery – an inassimilable foreign pest – and his commitment to the established procedures of the academic discipline of history, force him into taking a negative view of this development as a break with tradition. Althusserianism has become possible because of a decline in standards in higher education. It is a good question as to who is the real elitist, Althusser or Thompson?

(i) Thompson and 'orthodox' Marxism

There is no such thing as 'orthodox Marxism'. All 'orthodoxies' – Kautsky's, Lukács's, Stalin's – are particular theoretical constructions culled out of the possibilities within the complex whole of Marx and Engels's discourse. Thompson has every right to call himself and to be a Marxist – he is as heterodox as I am and no less. Those who see him as the saviour of the traditional landscape of Marxist theory from the ravages of Althusserianism had better look closely at how he does it – they will find as little left of what they purport to value.

Thompson poses the threat of Althusser to a supposedly established Marxist tradition:

> Althusser and his acolytes challenge, centrally, historical materialism itself. They do not offer to modify it but to displace it. . . .
> And if (as I suppose) Althusserian Marxism is not only an idealism but has many of the attributes of a theology, then what is at issue, within the Marxist tradition, is the defence of reason itself. (p. 126)

Stirring stuff. But the reason being defended – from within the Marxist tradition – is not *Marxist* reason but 'reason' itself. Nor is the 'historical materialism' at issue the Marxist theory of social relations and their development, rather it is the discipline of history guided by certain 'intuitions' on the part of Marx. Materialism in historical writing can be traced back beyond Marx in Thompson's genealogy to Vico. Marx's writings provide historians with 'hypotheses' (p. 258) which can be used to organise and be tested in historical research.

Thompson is happy to make historical materialism a humanistic discipline whose knowledge is different in nature from the natural sciences:

In this sense I am ready to agree that the attempt to designate history as a 'science' has always been unhelpful and confusing. If Marx and, even more, Engels sometimes fell into this error, then we may apologise, but we should not confuse the claim with their actual procedures. Marx certainly knew, also, that history was a Muse, and that the 'humanities' construct knowledges. (p. 231)

I doubt that Marx would have been so obliging as to concur. He would doubtless have been somewhat shocked by the identity effected between historical materialism as a theory of social relations and historiography. Marx clearly regarded historical materialism as a theoretical science whose methods and discoveries were at par with those of Moleschott's bio-energetics or Darwin's theory of natural selection (both of which influenced the formulations of *Capital*). This duality of the knowledges of Man versus knowledge of nature is alien to Marx's theory, although part and parcel of one line of defence of orthodox historiography as knowledge. Let that pass, Marxism is about to concede other territories nearer to its heartlands.

Thompson concurs with the despised Althusser in certain rather important matters: 'We must commence, at once, by agreeing that *Capital* is not a work of "history"' (p. 249), and that, 'it is true that in *Capital* "history" is introduced to provide exemplification and illustration for a structure of theory which is not derived from this discipline. However, reluctantly, we must go half-way towards the positions of Althusser and Balibar.' (p. 257) But what matters, therefore, in *Capital* is the historical work which is the source of hypotheses for historical research. The apparent primary objects of *Capital* are nothing but a false road. Marx's contestation of bourgeois Political Economy and his production of the theory of the capitalist mode of production as a response led him profoundly astray. Marx inherited the economism of his opponents, he mistakenly conceived of the economic as a 'first order activity' isolable in scientific abstraction and capable of giving rise to laws which would express the direction of development of society as a whole. This creates a 'structuralism' in which an aspect of the totality unconditionally determines the whole. It leads to a static conception of social relations: 'There is an important sense in which the movement of Marx's thought, in the *Grundrisse*, is locked inside a *static anti-historical structure*.' (pp. 252–3) This closed system of economic laws leads to all the difficulties Marxism has encountered at the hands of its critics:

> So we are forced to agree with seven generations of critics:
> *Capital* is a mountainous inconsistency. As pure Political
> Economy it may be faulted for introducing external categories:
> its laws cannot be verified, and its 'predictions' were wrong. (p.
> 257)

Thompson concedes the territory Marxist economists and sociologists have been battling to defend against the conventional wisdom of the 1950s without losing a hair.

Capital is doomed because its method of analysis of economic relations through categories in abstraction contradicts the nature of historical research. Marx's 'structuralist' concept of totality is rejected: 'Political Economy cannot show capital*ism* as "capital in the totality of its relations": it has no language or terms to do this. *Only a historical materialism* which could bring all activities and relations *within a coherent view* could do this.' (p. 254) That 'view', however, is not theoretical, it is the synoptic presentation of the real whole through its documentation. *Capital* is rejected in favour of Marx's 'intuitions':

> But historical materialism has found that Marx had a most
> profound intuition, an intuition which in fact *preceded* the
> *Grundrisse*: that the logic of capitalist process has found
> expression within all the activities of a society, and exerted a
> determining pressure on its development and form: hence
> entitling us to speak of capitalism or capitalist societies. (p. 254)

Totality as a concept, as mode of production, is to be rejected in favour of the *real* totality present in history to be discovered by historical research.

At the same time Thompson wishes to retain the notion of 'structure' (p. 302) and also the concept of 'exploitation' (p. 250). He will use both as and where convenient in his hypothetically guided historical research and discard them where they don't suit the evidence. That concepts like 'exploitation' have theoretical conditions in the rejected notion of mode of production is of no moment to him. 'Exploitation' requires (if it is to be more than a moral category) the concept of 'value' and that requires the economy to be conceived as a totality or closed system governed by the necessities of distribution of labour-time.

Likewise, the supposition of a totality in the real – of social relations expressive of an inner and all pervasive determinative principle – is not exactly an a-theoretical notion, something the historian just happened to 'pick up' in the course of his observations. This notion of a *real* totality – of which history can give us a 'coherent view' – is a theoretical device whereby other concepts of totality are attacked and displaced. It is a *concept* and one which needs defending theoretically. Thompson fails to develop the argument, but his conception of totality in history is remarkably similar to a certain reading of Hegel. Thompson's silence on Althusser's critique of the 'expressive' totality is interesting, since it is this category which is at the centre of the latter's critique of historicism. It is the co-presence of the elements as a single whole and their development as a whole which makes possible the pertinence of chronological time, this time reveals the successive 'presences' of the totality and such a totality makes pertinent the question of the co-existence of phenomena. It also justifies the category of 'experience' (Hegel gives it an important place in his system); experience is possible because the real exists as presence.

For Thompson history is a matter of 'finding out', but no definite enquiry can 'find out' this real totality which is so central to his category of capitalism. It is presupposed in his method and *if* such a totality were indeed to exist it would still require to be conceptualised and defended as such, for it would be all-pervasive and incapable of demonstration by reference to particular bodies of evidence or hypotheses. As an 'intuition' which organises historical research it is safe, it does not need defending because all 'intuitions' are at par with one another. What is valued in an 'intuition' is the 'results' it makes possible in the form of research measured against tests of evidence. In this ideology of the historical scholar the theoretical conditions of knowledge are given secondary status, as are the categories in terms of which the significance of its results are assessed (these become 'values'). This ideology survives because of its *contempt* for the theory it uses and not because of its capacity to do without it.

Thompson re-charts the intellectual terrain of Marxism to suit this notion of historical research:

> The homeland of Marxist theory remains where it has always
> been, the real human object, in all its manifestations (past and
> present) which object cannot be known in one theoretical *coup
> d'oeil* (as though theory could swallow reality in one gulp) but
> only through distinct disciplines, informed by unitary concepts.
> These disciplines or practices meet at each other's borders,
> exchange concepts, converse, correct each others' errors. Philo-
> sophy may (and must) monitor, refine and assist the conver-
> sation. (p. 236)

Philosophy is placed firmly in its role as underlabourer to the
'disciplines'. It may perform that role as long as it threatens nothing
in this happy division of labour. The disciplines are linked by
'unitary concepts' but these concepts *have no unity among
themselves*, precisely because Thompson denies any autonomy to
the work of formulating concepts which are the conditions of the
possibility for *questions*. But certain questions cannot be asked if
this intellectual division of labour is to be preserved. For a start:
what is 'the real human object, in all its manifestations'? Man is not
an *object* but a concept (a point to which we will return): human
animals do not necessarily (*sans concept*) form a unity in their
attributes and activities. Hence the problem of the possible *non-
unity* of those very 'manifestations', the dispersion of the space of
the 'real' object in which the disciplines meet. Thompson unifies his
field of phenomena by a concept of human essence but he refuses to
elaborate that concept to the point where it could be defended.

Thompson's division of labour is designed precisely to preserve
the 'disciplines' *against* philosophy or theoretical practice. This
preservation is necessary since much of their 'evidence' depends on
theoretical categories and notions of proof, and once this circumstance is raised as a question and those categories and notions
subjected to theoretical dispute this 'evidence' ceases to be
evidential. But, it may be objected, Thompson assures us that
'historical logic' is a rigorous test of concepts. Marxist hypotheses
are to be tested in the court of historical research: 'For historical
knowledge, this court lies within the discipline of history and
nowhere else.' (pp. 236–7) But Thompson's court tries not *concepts*
but propositions derived from them with reference to particular
bodies of evidence. The result is like telling psychoanalysis that its
concepts are about to be tested (objectively, of course) in the

laboratory of Professor Eysenck. Thompson has rejected those concepts which cannot be so tested and relegated them to the junk-yard of concepts irrelevant to the analysis of social relations. Mode of production has gone, and I'm afraid, although Thompson neglects to mention this, so have most of the concepts of Marxist economic theory associated with it – value, surplus value, laws of tendency, etc.

However, these concepts have been dispatched not by reference to Thompson's court (which cannot try them) but by *philosophical arguments*. For Thompson has been engaging in 'theoretical practice' – he has had to – but only enough of it before scuttling back to the real homeland of historical materialism. He hasn't stayed on the enemy's terrain long enough to fight the decisive battle. If the concept of mode of production (a totality of social relations determined by the economic level which internalises its conditions of existence and effects) is untenable – and Barry Hindess and I have argued far more cogently than Thompson *why* this is so – then the central organising concept of the Marxist analysis of social relations is displaced. It needs to be replaced by *another concept* – one which is not burdened by ontological suppositions which exceed what it can demonstrate. Thompson ignores this need for theoretical work. He is happy to suppose a totality *in* the real, which in its *reality* secures the possibility of his historical research (his 'finding out'). This supposition is to exceed his means of demonstration (his 'court') and yet is the condition for its functioning.

Thompson, having challenged the concept of mode of production and having set up history as a poor man's queen of the sciences, rediscovers economics one hundred pages later:

> [W]e may first offer an apology to Marxist economists. The theory of mode of production belongs, very properly, within their own conceptual system. It is proper that it should be interrogated and refined. The continuing debates among econ-omists may well be significant, and historians hope to be helped by their findings. (p. 348)

How the poor devils can do anything, if they take Thompson seriously, except pick up the ruins of *Capital* and see what's left, escapes me. Thompson here seeks to assure us that in rejecting Althusser he is not tearing the guts out of *Capital* – we have his fiat but no arguments. The categories of Marxist economic theory require as their theoretical condition the very notion of totality Thompson claims he wants to reject. He calls Althusserianism a 'caricature', but, in its literal sense, a caricature sums up the essence of a face. *Reading Capital* accurately reproduces some of the main lines of argument in *Capital* and validly criticises others. Thompson cannot sensibly set himself against the Marxist economists because he would then have no 'disciplines' left with which to parallel history (sociology is clearly too contaminated to be rehabilitated). But he cannot really offer them anything except tolerance, his whole conception of historical materialist practice is encapsulated by the discipline of history.

Althusser, we are solemnly told (pp. 355, 362), equates mode of production and social formation. How it is possible to read *Reading Capital* and fail to notice that one of its main objectives is to separate those concepts remains a mystery to me. Althusser argues that mode of production is a *concept* (a determinate form of abstraction) and cannot be equated with concrete social relations. All social formations consist of more than one mode of production, and the concepts of the various modes require to be applied in a distinct level of (theoretical) analysis. As a *concept*, the forms of causality postulated at the level of the mode of production are not those of concrete social formations, the order of concepts in abstraction does not *correspond* to the order of the real, concepts are a means of analysis of the real and not a picture of the real itself. The complex relations of the real cannot be present to observational knowledge. Thompson insists on treating Althusser's concept of mode of production as if it were a 'model' or reality itself.

Althusser's failure is quite different from the one criticised. It is not a failure to separate the two categories – mode of production and social formation. Rather the problem is that, for all Althusser's claims to the contrary, there is no way in which his concept of mode of production allows the construction of differential concepts of social formations. The concept's central properties would have to be displaced in the process. But this is another matter and requires different grounds of criticism from those offered by Thompson: Barry Hindess and I have carried out this critical work in *Mode of*

Production and Social Formation. But then Thompson claims that 'life is too short' (p. 196) to take our work seriously.

Thompson insists that Marx does *not* equate mode of production and social formation. 'But we must say at once that Marx never pretended, when he was writing *Capital*, that he was writing the history of capital*ism*.' (p. 249) Marx certainly did not pretend to write the *history* of capitalism, he allowed for different national routes and conditions for its development. *Capital* is, as Thompson knows, not primarily concerned with the genesis of capital – the chapters on genesis are merely 'illustrative'. *Capital* is not a history, but that is because Marx claimed to be writing capitalism's *future*. The words of the preface to the first German edition confirm this with chilling exactness:

> *De te fabula narratur!* . . . It is a question of these laws themselves, of these tendencies working with iron necessity toward inevitable results. The country which is more developed industrially only shows, to the less developed, the image of its own future.

To tell us that when Marx wrote of *Capital* that in it 'the economic formation of society is viewed as a process of natural history' and that men appear in it as 'personifications of economic categories' he was writing 'with his tongue firmly in his cheek' (p. 340) is little short of absurd. Thompson is well aware, and correctly so, of Marx's admiration for Darwin: to view society as a natural history was not a cause for irony but pride. Just as to view material production and the division of labour as a social 'metabolism', an 'exchange of matter' (*Stoffswechsel*), after Moleschott was also a deliberate borrowing from the biological sciences – and one persisted in despite Moleschott's vulgar materialism. Marx wrote his preface in deadly earnest – he was teaching his countrymen a lesson – and he insisted that the capitalist mode of production was the inner essence of capitalism working according to economic laws which could be studied with a rigour directly comparable to the natural sciences. I happen to think and to have argued (in *Marx's Capital and Capitalism Today*) that both Marx's conception of capitalism and of the method by which it should be studied are untenable, but I would defend both against Thompson's excursion into 'what Marx really meant'. A series of 'intuitions' about processes of capitalist development whose real features are to be uncovered by historians' research was not the legacy he sought to give to posterity. Thompson husks Marxist theory, its central work, *Capital*, takes up the shell and casts aside the kernel – hypotheses culled from *Capital* are to be used, where relevant in historical research.

(ii) Epistemology

It is necessary to consider what this 'historical research' offers us as a substitute for the untenable claims of Marxist theory. But in order to do so we must engage in some preliminary discussion of epistemology. 'Historical research' is a process of 'finding out', of measuring hypotheses against the evidence. This is the alternative to Althusser's conception of the knowledge process as the 'appropriation of the concrete in thought'.

There is no way in which I can or would want to defend the propositions of Althusser's epistemology – Barry Hindess and I have argued in *Mode of Production and Social Formation* why *all* attempts to construct a necessary relation between two distinct general realms, knowledge and being, in which the former appropriates or corresponds to the latter are doomed to failure. But Thompson's attack on Althusser's work reveals a depth of ignorance which cannot be disregarded or go unchallenged. It also reveals his conception of the knowledge process which is central to his discipline of history.

Thompson assures us: 'I don't propose to counter Althusser's paradigm of knowledge-production with an alternative one of my own.' (p. 205) But that is exactly what he does do in the course of the critical questions he addresses to Althusser. He sets out the permissible methods of knowledge in the human sciences. Thompson asks, how does Althusser's mechanism of the 'knowledge effect' work? Thompson confesses he is unable to understand Althusser on this question. The short answer is that it doesn't; it is the empty metaphor and silence at the heart of Althusser's epistemology. It occupies that point (the condition of the knowledge-being relation) at which *all* epistemologies degenerate into silence, incoherence or dogma. Thompson is capable of recognising Althusser's failure but not what it signifies. He immediately asks why Althusser does not explain what the raw materials of knowledge are, where they come from and how they are presented to be known. He contends that he is not asking for 'guarantees', but interprets a guarantee in a very limited sense as being a means of demonstrating formally an identity or one-to-one correspondence between real objects and their conceptual representations. The issue for him is not such an identity, but the method of producing adequately valid knowledge.

But to ask his question is to posit the need for a 'guarantee' in a larger and more pertinent sense. Virtually no epistemological doctrine has ever asked for or proffered a 'guarantee' in the limited sense of Thompson's definition. What Thompson seeks, as a condition of Althusser's epistemology meeting the standards of philosophical rigour that he imposes on it, is a general doctrine of being which explains thereby the possibility of a relation between the knowing subject and the known object. Althusser ignores 'reality': he fails to characterise the knowledge-being relation in materialist terms, in terms of the real processes which make it possible. Thompson is seeking a characterisation of the essential attributes of the object as a condition of validity of a doctrine of method. But this is to pre-determine in the most complete way what is to be known. Knowledge must pre-exist itself as its own condition.

Althusser's epistemology (in one of its contradictory aspects) sought to avoid this problem by refusing 'guarantees' on the one hand, and by *not* assigning essential attributes to the being to be known. The real is interiorised to knowledge within the forms of knowledge. Knowledge has access to reality only through the distinct theoretically constructed objects of the sciences. Experiment is (following Bachelard) a process of 'materialisation of theory'. Althusser's epistemology denies the very pertinence of Thompson's demand. Generalities I are *always* within theory; they are already definite organised bodies of conceptual knowledge. To ask for the 'origin' of knowledge is to pose a problem of infinite regress. Thompson assumes that GI, the 'raw materials' of theoretical practice, are *raw materials* in the sense of representations of real objects on which theory works: 'Since theory disallows any active appropriation of the external world in the only way possible (by active engagement or dialogue with its evidence) then *this whole world must be assumed*. The "raw materials" (GI) which arrive are simply taken as *given*.' (pp. 227–8) Generalities I are *never* given, they are the product of discourse and interiorised within theory. Althusser denies immediate access to the 'external world' *at any level*, all social 'experience' is conditional upon categories and definite techniques, it is also implicated in the imaginary. We have no Ur-level of access to the real, and we can make no assumptions as to what it is 'really' like or what its effects upon knowledge are.

Thompson, however, has just such a means of unifying the external world as object to the subject of knowledge and of explaining its mode of presentation to the subject, the category of 'experience'. Doctrines of knowledge are really a futile superfluity (this is why Thompson feels comfortable in claiming not to offer one), we already know the fundamental nature of the real and of knowledge through our 'experience' of it. Thompson appeals – against epistemology – to a supported experiential-intuitional level to legitimate his own conception of knowledge.

Experience is:

> a category which, however imperfect it may be, is indispensable to the historian, since it comprises the mental and emotional response, whether of an individual or social group, to many inter-related events or to many repetitions of the same kind of event. (p. 199)

Althusser ignores the '*dialogue* between social being and social consciousness' (p. 201): 'Experience arises spontaneously within social being, but it does not arise without thought; it arises because men and women . . . are rational and they think about what is happening to themselves and their world.' (p. 200) All knowledge is modelled on this practical experience and reason:

> There can be no means of deciding the 'adequacy or inadequacy' of *knowledge* (as against the special cases of logic, mathematics, etc.) unless one supposes procedures (a 'dialogue' of practice) devised to establish the correspondence of this knowledge to properties 'inscribed in' the real. (p. 209)[3]

Thompson has forgotten his promise not to commit the sin of epistemology. But more is to follow. Practical experience and reason are possible, knowledge of the real is possible, *because of the nature and action of that reality itself*. The relation between knowledge and the real:

> may take place not *on any terms which thought prescribes* but in

ways which are determined by the properties of the real object; the properties of reality determine both the appropriate procedures of thought (that is, their 'adequacy or inadequacy') and its product. Herein lies the 'dialogue' between consciousness and being. (p. 209)

Herein also lies the possibility of Thompson's 'historical knowledge' which consists in 'finding out' what really happened. This 'dialogue' takes place *within men*:

Thought and being inhabit a single space, which space is ourselves. Even as we think we also hunger and hate, we sicken or we love, and consciousness is intermixed with being; even as we contemplate the 'real' we experience our own palpable reality. (p. 210)

The real object of knowledge determines both the possibility and the nature of knowledge of it. It does so in ways which make its action knowable to us as truth. (How convenient! How providential that reality should make the world in empiricism's image and give us confirmation of the fact.) Knowledge and its object are united in the knowing subject. The dialogue of consciousness and being is located within the 'single space' which is Man. It is because of this identity that knowledge through 'experience' is possible: 'experience' is consciousness of being and reasoning upon it. Subject and object ultimately share the same nature, what men are is (potentially) accessible to their consciousness because they are capable of being – in the full sense – the authors of their acts. If they did not have this capacity we could not be so sure that 'experience' is (potentially) adequate to its object.

The locus of this epistemological doctrine *manqué* is the category of the human, of Man. It is Man beyond any category, the 'reality' of humanity and our 'palpable' experience of ourselves, that we are referred to. But who is this stranger we are supposed to recognise in ourselves? Real men? But they come in many guises, from the Gas Board to the Gestapo. They say and do things which have no parallel, things which to Thompson's 'rational mind' form 'the greater part of the history of ideas' which is 'a history of freaks' (p. 195). Are these 'freaks' practitioners of 'reason'? If so that reason is at once reasonable and freakish. Or is reason a matter of the right values? Thompson waxes lyrical about the practical knowledges of

ordinary men, 'the sailor "knows" his seas' (p. 199). Of course
sailors do, but they also know where not to go in order to avoid the
sea monsters and they know the fate that awaits the poor fool who
sets out into the Atlantic to sail to Cathay. These things form a
single 'knowledge', confirmed a hundred times over by 'experience'. Likewise, witch hunters 'know' their witches, they can smell
them a mile off and can search out their palpable marks with
unerring accuracy.

As the conceptual support this epistemological doctrine which
calls beyond theory to 'experience', Thompson supposes a universal
human subject. This being has the same essential attributes in all of
its incarnations: it is unitary within the 'single space' of its self-
experience, and all the members of its class have the common
faculties of 'consciousness' and 'reason'. These faculties have a
generality which transcends any definite forms of their organisation: throughout the ages there has been 'reason' as such.
Sociology may be a discipline beneath contempt, the new Dismal
Science, but at least the best of its practitioners have sought to
dispel the myth of this being. Althusser, Derrida, Foucault and
Lacan may be denizens of that fashion-ridden City of the Night,
Paris, but they have sought to make the human subject a problem
for investigation, rather than a datum to be celebrated and made
the unquestioned basis of explanation of discourses and social
relations.

Thompson tells us he 'commenced to reason' in his thirty-third
year (p. i). 'Reason' is contrasted with 'theology'. But what is this
'reason' without determinate premises or conceptual conditions? It
can be nothing other than 'human' thought itself. Thompson
requires the philosophical concept of 'humanity' to sustain his
discourse. It is that notion I find either empty or impossible, not
because I dislike men but because I want to understand them. In my
thirty-third year, having begun my intellectual life deeply committed to philosophical humanism, I confess that the one piece of
knowledge I feel any certainty about is that men can say *anything*
and consider it reasonable.

Thompson in challenging Althusser's 'anti-humanism' appeals to
the *reality* of our experience. His imaginary woman cries out 'I am
not a bloody thing!' (p. 344) Whoever supposed she was?
Thompson takes the side of humanity against the monstrous
philosophy of Althusser, he thinks of Althusser as a Dalek crying

'exterminate' at the very sight of men (p. 337). It is his misfortune to suppose that all theoretical work is the actualisation of values, that the problematisation of the philosophical *concept* of man betokens a desire to eliminate the members of the species *homo sapiens*. I cannot think Thompson can be proud of this sleight of hand.

Thompson's appeal to the *reality* of our experience has a long philosophical pedigree. When Kierkegaard protested the reality of *his* experience against its consumption as a fragment of a moment in Hegel's dialectic, or when Sartre in *The Problem of Method* protested against vulgar Marxism's appropriation of experience in 'objective' interests, they protested the appropriation of the *meaning* of that experience to the subject, its incorporation as an effect of causes external to the subject. Thompson is not concerned to assert the (unquestionable) subjective validity of experience, its immediateness to self and mediateness to Other; he wishes to establish an active faculty of experience common to subjects.

The 'anti-humanism' I am concerned to defend does not seek to *abolish* men, or to appropriate the experience of subjectivity, but to problematise the category of subject. It does not challenge the reality of 'experience', but asks what are its conditions, its forms and its effects. It challenges the notion of subject as a unitary self-experience, a presence-to-self in the single and continuous space of consciousness. It is this very presence which makes both the subject and a stable, continuous body of experience possible. In humanist philosophies the subject is a unity as consciousness and as agent, it is capable of knowing itself (through reflection on that unity) and of being the source of its actions. It is this centredness in consciousness that philosophical anti-humanism in its various forms (not only Althusser but Nietzsche and Freud) challenges.

Anti-humanism's challenge consists, on the one hand, in the construction of a new *concept* of the subject. The subject is not an originary unity but a *trace*, a construction in language, a centred-ness of statements (whether spoken or thought). It is one (crucial) aspect of psychic like, but it is not the whole. On the other hand, the challenge is a rejection of the notion that human individuals can be thought of exclusively as subjects, in any sense of that term. The human being is not a subject, a centred and inclusive consciousness. This is not least because unconscious thoughts and desires interrupt centred speech – the unconscious refuses to be one of the additional predicates 'of' a person. When Lacan says, deliberately punning *Cogito ergo sum*, 'I think where I am not, therefore I am where I do not think' (*Ecrits*, p. 166), he is not engaging in Parisian perversity but struggling to express something which is vital to the understanding of subjectness and of what lies beyond the centredness of statements.

Without the support of a stable presence-to-itself of consciousness, 'experience' is threatened with dispersion. Once we attach a question to the 'I', posing it as an effect by no means singular or stable (although by no means without effects), then the solidity of 'experience' as a something *of* the subject becomes in turn problematic. Thompson's knowing subject is the pivot of his knowledge process, it is man's capacity to know 'his' products in 'his' experience which makes historical knowledge possible.

Thompson assumes an evident unity 'experience'. But what is at stake is what counts as 'experience' in different discourses and practices. Thus he would not appreciate experimental psychologists' conceptions of what validly fell under the category.

'Experience' has been saved from the problems of 'consciousness', has been rendered stable in Positivist epistemologies to the extent that it is conceived as non-subjective. Only definite statements about observables, objective representations of replicable experiences, are permitted as the data of science. This 'experience' – intersubjective and impersonal – deliberately excludes the mass of human thoughts, concerns and perceptions Thompson wishes to signify by the term. 'Experience' as the basis of a defensible epistemology rests – as Carnap shows – on the possibility of a pure 'observation language'. The problem is the notion of a *language* of observables, of its grammar and syntax. It poses the problem of a means of unifying a field of observational data, of connecting them without recourse to such categories as 'judgment' or the problematic intervention of an active, selective, knowing subject. For Thompson a rigorous empiricist like Carnap is as much a Gradgrind in the face of the 'real object' as Althusser.

Thompson's 'experience' is grounded on the supposition of that 'real human object', the supposition that human social life forms an intelligible totality. This category transcends any of the means of demonstration Thompson considers *tests* of validity, indeed the uses to which he puts his tests rest on this category. Consciousness and being are determined in their relation 'by the properties of the real object'. That intelligible totality is by no means simple and immediate:

> The relationship between thought and its object now becomes so exceedingly complex and mediated; and, moreover, the resulting historical knowledge establishes relations between phenomena which could never be seen, felt or experienced by the actors in these ways at the time, and it organises the findings according to concepts and within categories which were unknown to the women and men whose actions make up the object of study – all these difficulties are so immense that 'real' history and historical knowledge are things totally distinct. (p. 211)

Historical knowledge is, however, still possible, still knowledge *of* the real because that reality forms an intelligible totality. Human existence is a totality in each of the successive moments of its existence and the totality of those moments (history) is an intelligible and inter-communicating whole. *That* is the condition for Thompson's knowledge process, *that* unifies human 'experience' and makes the category tenable as both record and means of historical knowledge. This is what Althusser means by the couple, humanism-historicism. In one aspect of his work Hegel *argued* for and conceptualised the supposition Thompson must rely on. Thompson dare not give it rigorous shape if he is to insist as he does on the 'empirical' (as opposed to 'empiricist') nature of his knowledges. He cannot dispense with it none the less. We will now turn to the practice of knowledge he offers us in the shape of historical research.

(iii) History

Thompson writes passionately to defend the discipline of history and the practice of historical writing. He feels threatened in his very right to engage in that practice by Althusserian philosophical criticism. Thompson is no mere antiquarian, his work has always been chosen with reference to politics. But, as we have seen, he does conceive the central practice of 'historical materialism' to be historical research. Marxist theory may produce hypotheses which guide research, but Marxist historiography shares a common discipline with other modes of writing history.

History is an *empirical* discipline, it is concerned with real bodies of phenomena, it is not to be confused, as Althusser does, with empiric*ism*. Althusser 'cannot understand (or must mispresent) the character of those empirical procedures which are elaborated, within different disciplines, not only to interrogate "facts" but to ensure that they reply, not in the investigator's voice, but in their own voices' (p. 225). This empirical discipline encounters *given* (p. 219) facts: 'The historical evidence is there, in its primary form, not to disclose its own meaning, but to be interrogated by minds trained in a discipline of attentive disbelief.' (pp. 220–1)

Thompson is right to say that the writing of history could not be an empiric*ist* practice. This is because empiricism as an epistemology posits an impossible *knowledge* process. It supposes a reality which is auto-significatory, which contains the knowledge of itself present-to-observation. The task of the knowing subject is *recognition*, the determination among the observables it encounters of signification and order in the real. The operations of knowledge are conceived as removing impediments to the recognition of that given significance and order, and not as constitutive of it. Hence Althusser's characterisation of empiricism as an abstractive process, extracting from what is given its essence which is knowledge. Thompson castigates this conception as a 'caricature' (p. 198), worthy of St Thomas perhaps but not of Locke (p. 385). Thompson, like his source for this criticism, Leszek Kolakowski, simply ignores the fact that Althusser explicitly says that 'empiricism' in his usage is a concept for the *consequences* of many diverse philosophical positions, it is not a name for a particular school in the history of ideas. Further, almost all epistemological discourse is an attempt to retreat from, avoid or ameliorate these consequences. Althusser does not suppose Aquinas's and Locke's epistemological doctrines to be the same; they differ radically in the means to knowledge and the tests of validity to be imposed on it, but not in the consequence of conceiving knowledge as a recognition (involving abstractive procedures) of a knowledge present in the real. Thompson's own account of his 'empirical procedures' shows that he shares this consequence with his illustrious forebears. Historical knowledge is conceived as the abstractive generation of significations from within a given reality itself, concepts merely facilitate the abstractive process and in no sense constitute the field of the known.

Historical writing is a practice predominantly conducted under the sign of empiricist epistemology. Empiricism may be impossible as a practice, but for many historians it is the doctrine of knowledge which threatens what they actually do least. Thompson's remarks in which he outlines the object and procedure of the historian's practice reveal clearly why this is so. Historical writing has a dual object, certain hitherto existing phenomena which are accessible, through their signification in documents or other artefacts. Its 'facts' which are 'given' (in Thompson's sense) are the materials it works on, records, documents, artefacts: objects which contain significations and require interpretation. Through that interpretation the hitherto existing is reconstructed. Thompson says: 'historical "facts" are "produced" by appropriate discipline from the evidential facts' (p. 291). These disciplines serve to reveal one order of facts present in another, existential facts are constituted from evidential facts. Hence the play on words in Thompson's statements quoted above between a facticity which cannot disclose its meaning – which requires the extractive interrogation of 'attentive disbelief' – and yet will at the end of that interrogation speak in its own voice. The existential facts thus extracted are a measure of all the discourses placed upon them, *they* are the judges in the court. They are the primary element in the process of knowledge and reveal the falsity of (inappropriate) significations placed upon them: Thompson agrees with his arch-enemy Karl Popper (p. 232) that the 'disciplinary court of appeal' is staffed by falsificationalists. He must also agree with a consequence of Popper's position (one that the latter constructed his work in order to avoid) that the reality against which theories are measured is intelligible or recognisable independent of those theories, observations or facts are not conditional upon definite theories.

Thompson proposes to use theories to account for and to attribute significance to existential facts. Theories are measured against 'the very givenness of facts, the determinate properties they present to the practitioner' (p. 219). But what are the *given* facts? They are 'evidential' in Thompson's sense, that is they are documents, records, etc., with 'determinate properties'. Theories must be converted into *propositions* which can be measured against those bodies of evidential material. The test is whether the propositions match evidential significations or patterns of relation between and consistency in the documents. As a method of interpreting documents it can only be assessed by its 'results' (Thompson agrees that history is no science). As an operationalisation of theories like those contained in Marx's *Capital* or Freud's *Civilisation and its Discontents* the results are little short of a disaster.

In Thompson's conception of the historian's practice it is certain ('given') materials which happen to be available and from which a selection is made which constitute its object and determine its procedures. The theories from which propositions are derived are external to these materials and secondary, they are *means* to knowledge. Hypotheses are framed to test the significance and consistency of the given materials. Hypotheses can be dispensed with if disconfirmed with reference to a certain selected body of evidential materials, but it is possible that they may be revived and re-utilised in relation to another such selection. The relation between theory and evidence is a matter for the historian to determine in each case. What matters is that the facts speak in their own voices at the end, that the bodies of evidential materials tell all they have to say in the most consistent and intelligible fashion. (*All* theory is impoverished against the − intelligible − richness of the primary materials. Althusser is merely the most blatant example, a wretched concept-smith who has stepped out of his station as underlabourer.)

What we have here is the classic historian's prioritisation of documents; they define, in defining the object, the unity and nature of the practice itself. This prioritisation is not mistaken. Separated from the evidentialisation of documents as testimonies to hitherto existing phenomena, historiography ceases to have any unity as a practice. As such it is united by object and method, but it has no unity of significance. Documents form a diverse mass relating to many practices and activities: there are potentially as many 'histories' as there are grounds for selecting and constructing bodies of evidential testimony, histories of art, administration, archery, etc. This is neither a problem nor a source of concern for the antiquarian.

But such a dispersion could never sustain a 'historical materialism'. Thompson has justified the centrality of the historian's practice to Marxism because for him it is the point of unity of the discrete disciplines. Historiography is the core discipline of the human sciences because it offers the entire past of humanity as a 'laboratory' in which to test hypotheses: '"history" is a good laboratory, because process, eventuation, is present within every moment of the evidence, testing every hypothesis in an outcome, providing results for every human experiment that has ever been conducted' (p. 240). Every one except, it might be objected, the one we are striving to bring to fruition. This laboratory is possible, pertinent to us and our 'experiments', because the difference between past and present has no ontological significance: 'To suppose that a "present" by moving into a "past", thereby changes its ontological status is to misunderstand both past and present.' (p. 232)[4] This continuity exists because both past and present are alike manifestations of a common and interconnecting course of human action: 'Our knowledge (we hope) is not thereby imprisoned within the past. It helps us know who we are, why we are here, what human possibilities have been disclosed, and as much as we can know of the logic and forms of social process.' (p. 239)

Thompson's position is sustained by two key suppositions which we have had cause to consider before:

(a) that human activities form a single intelligible real totality at each historical moment, hence all the possible 'histories' inter-penetrate;
(b) that the moments of this history form a single intercommuni-cating chain of significances, the history of humanity forms an intelligible whole.

Social relations form a totality and this is ultimately intelligible as (significant) *human action*. Representations, knowledges and sig-nificatory practices form a single human 'culture'. The referent of this totalisation, the condition of this unity, is the notion of 'man'; a being constant in its essential attributes and potential, the origin and measure of this whole process. What saves Thompson's 'historical materialism' from antiquarian irrelevance is a philo-sophically saturated humanism.

The pertinence of historical writing is that it is a way of reflecting and continuing this culture. The historian selects according to his values from the values enunciated by actors in the past, he attributes significance to their actions, and he hopes to communi-cate them to us and to others not yet living – to pass on the torch:

Our vote will change nothing. And yet in another sense, it may change everything. For we are saying that these values, and not those other values, are the ones which make this history

meaningful to *us*, and that these are the values which we intend
to enlarge and sustain in our own present. If we succeed then we
reach back into history and endow it with our own meanings.
What we may hope is that the men and women of the future will
reach back to us, will affirm and renew our meanings, and make
our history intelligible within their own present tense. (p. 234)

Thompson's history is theoretically saturated. It finds its unity as
object and its value as a practice in concepts which transcend what
it can establish by the 'empirical procedures' it sets up as tests of
valid knowledge. These procedures or tests are conducted within a
theoretical field. This field is assumed rather than argued for. For
all Thompson's insistence on the evidence and 'finding out', the
procedures which purport to determine what is signified in bodies
of documents rely for their relevance on theoretical arguments as to
their contemporary value. There is no 'evidence' as such (as given);
evidentialisation is a conceptual process. A non-antiquarian history
requires a philosophy of history.

Thompson's unarticulated philosophy supposes that men are the
'subjects of history', that is, that history is ultimately intelligible
(with due account for objective conditions and circumstances) as
the resultant of men acting to realise 'values'. If that were indeed
the case then the communication of 'values' to future generations
would be a legitimate objective of Marxists, it would act on the
decisive process by which history is made. Thompson's men must
act together and be able to *realise* values in order to be subjects,
history would otherwise be the record of crossed purposes and
frustrated hopes. The historian's values are pertinent (they transcend the category of 'freaks') to the extent that they correspond to
those which motivate large groups of men and are capable of
having significance because of the resultants of those groups'
actions. Values are not merely ideas, nor are they merely a matter of
conscious choice: they actively express ways of living, and these
ways are part of the concrete totality which is social life.

Culture, tradition and class form a triad in Thompson's work.
Classes are human collectivities sharing common values, modes of
action and conditions of life. Their values are a response to their
conditions and a continuation of the traditions they inherit. The
Marxist historian has a role because he assists in the mediation of
tradition; he actively expresses the values of the working class and

participates in the continual re-making of its culture. It is now time to assess the political consequences of this conception of the practice of knowledge.

(iv) History and politics

Politics is thought in this triad as mass action, as action-in-tradition, as the continuing expression and development of the values of the collectivity. Marxist history mediates the successive incarnations of a subject, a collectivity of actors, a national working class. For this mediation to have political effect the members of this class must be capable of being the subjects of history, of acting to realise their values. Lukács resolved this question theoretically in *History and Class Consciousness* with a necessary dialectic inherent in the contradictions of capitalism. Thompson's conceptions of class and politics might appear to lead him in that direction. Thompson retains the conceptions of capitalism as a concrete totality harbouring certain essential contradictions, and for him this totality of human action, however reified and alienated, must, because it is made by men, be capable of transformation. But this transformation remains *in potentia*. Thompson does not posit theoretically a set of conditions which will create effective mass action mobilising the class as a whole around certain values. He says

> that every class struggle is at the same time a struggle over values; and that the project of Socialism is guaranteed BY NOTHING – certainly not by 'Science' or by Marxism-Leninism – but can find its own guarantees only by *reason* and an open *choice of values*. (p. 363)

Neither reason nor choice can be made the necessary or immediate effect of objective conditions. Thompson takes his humanism seriously, he refuses to aggregate the working class into a supra-subjective agent. But to the extent that he refuses to do this his humanist theory of historical continuity and change is threatened, men can only be the 'subjects of history' if they act in concert to achieve the actualisation of values.

Thompson is too honest and has seen the defeat of too many hopes to believe that victory awaits us in the effects of the *next* crisis. He refuses to commit himself to a facile evolutionary theory in which the subjective and the objective conditions for the realisation of class values coincide. That is to his credit, but it leaves his men as the 'subjects of history' waiting in the wings.

Thompson is left with three things, historical evocation, utopian exhortation and hope:

> as that the atomised and predatory logic of capitalism . . . can only be displaced by the alternative intentions and aspirations of a social consciousness which can (as empirically given historical fact) be shown to find partial and fragmented embodiment in the actual working-class movement. British history, over 150 years, has shown this alternative possibility to be waxing and waning and waxing again – not as *exactly the same* possibility, but as the same in terms of an alternative, socialist logic. ('Open Letter', *Poverty of Theory*, p. 147)

Thompson's 'historical materialism' is *political*: it has nothing in common with the kind of social history which is busy telling a Labour Movement which doesn't listen, or does so on ritual occasions and to learn nothing, about its grandfathers' lives and battles. It is political because it is ruthlessly selective of the 'traditions' and the values of the 'culture' it seeks to continue. Yet it needs the myth of a continuous cultural tradition. History is central to Thompson's Marxist politics, because that politics is thought as continuist and expressive – standing for the good old cause. Utopianism, the insistence on the possibility of a complete break which realises human potentialitics, is coupled with a (selectively constructed) traditionalism, this break will awaken and realise values which have all along been there.

This conception of the role of knowledge in politics is necessarily *a-stragetic*. It is a politics of the expression of values, of the husbanding of potentialities, of waiting for future possibilities: a politics within the realm of 'culture'. Thompson as guardian of a cultural 'tradition' is threatened by radical transformations which break this continuist practice, like the domestication of European Marxism and avant-garde culture. Thompson is surprised by the failure of the 'libertarian tradition' to become a major force in British politics, to occupy the 'vacuum' to the left of rightist social democracy. Thompson's practice of Marxism gives him no means to comprehend or to come to terms with this failure.

Thompson has no means to assess the extent of *our* problem: the conditions for a democratic socialism. The 'working class' Thompson writes the history of, selectively reflecting its values as tradition, is a declining *minority* of the population. Britain has more employees in banks and financial institutions than miners, more teachers than steelworkers, more waiters than car assembly workers. He can mediate no traditions or values to masses of people who must vote for, actively support or acquiesce in socialism if it is to have any choice of success. Thompson derides the 'piecemeal, softly-softly social engineering' (*Open Letter*, p. 177) he associates with Sir Karl Popper. I have no love of it but I suspect that Thompson would associate with it any programme of strategic reform. Socialism under existing political and economic conditions cannot be a revolutionary break, but a process of construction of non-commodity and co-operative social relations achieved *through and against* the existing forms of politics. The Labour Party remains central, it must be the primary vehicle on the Left because untransformed it constitutes one of the primary obstacles. Thompson's opposition of 'libertarianism' and 'statism' cannot come to terms with the specific 'statist' practices of the Labour governments since 1945. It cannot accept the need for a different practice of legislation and administration, it can only condemn.

Thompson's 'historical materialism' cannot serve to make socialism into policies and practices which can be fought for today with the forces at hand. Instead, it becomes an ideal to be upheld, the realisation of a new form of society. Thompson's insistence on the need for utopia basically refuses the kind of re-thinking of socialist practices and objectives required in contemporary Britain. We are confronted with a situation of severe political, economic and social constraints on the policies which could be implemented and with little prospect of their revolutionary decomposition. Thompson refuses to survey the forces and arenas socialist politics must work in if it is to succeed under existing conditions, for him our dismal present is a 'waning' period of socialist possibilities which 'active reason' must endure. Thompson is not, however, a political and cultural pessimist, his thought does not suffer from the sort of demobilising negativism one finds in Marcuse's *One Dimensional Man*. His motto is '*Eppur si muove!*' (p. 300), an insistence on human agency and creativity, and on the motive forces of his human practice, reason and values. Yes, Edward

Thompson, it does move. But the movement towards socialism involves more than 'human agency' *per se*: it involves definite forms of organisation, specific practices, policies which are no mere derivation of values, and so on. And it *moves* toward something other than a new society which is the realisation of 'values', it involves programmes for the construction of those specific institutions and social relationships which can work and can be attained against the resistance of other organised humans. 'Values' – democracy, equality, co-operation, 'from each according to his ability, to each according to his need', and so on – *always* transcend definite institutions. Our movement must have values, but, if they are to have any value, they must serve in the struggle for what definite institutions are attainable. Thompson's utopianism sets its face against *this* movement.

(v) Politics and morality

Thompson is right to insist on the limitations of theory, and to stress the role of what he calls 'morality' and 'values' in socialism. This is no paradox on my part. In my own way I have stressed the limitations of Marxist theory no less radically than Thompson. Thompson, however, seeks to throw the burden primarily on Althusser, and to posit a Marxist tradition of 'active reason'. I have tried to show the illusion of such a 'tradition', Thompson's dependence in fact on a certain kind of theoretical practice and his failure to defend it. Marxism is in desperate need of reconstruction. It is degenerating on the one hand into a series of sterile 'orthodoxies', and on the other into a cynical opportunism which unthinkingly retires those categories which appear to threaten parliamentary success. That reconstruction cannot leave much of the existing architecture of concepts intact, and it can only be done by theoretical work in the service of a politics which seeks to adapt our objectives and forms of struggle to 'current conditions.' Theory is necessary for this reason, we cannot merely leave the edifice of Marxist theory as a kind of cathedral we visit on ritual occasions.

The reason we cannot simply leave Marxist theory as it is is because, as 'scientific socialism', it has been the main carrier of the objectives and standards of judgment of our movement. Marxism has derided moralism. It has made the question of socialism an objective question; socialist social relations will exist because capitalism as a mode of production is riven with inherent contradictions which make the socialisation of the force of production necessary. The job of socialists is to organise the class struggle which is the political mediation of that contradiction. The character of socialist social relations is a question of future objective conditions on which it is idle and utopian to speculate. Now I agree with Thompson in rejecting 'scientific socialism': the victory of socialism is not given. But, and here I differ from him, I do not accept either that socialism is a distinct *form* of society, different from capitalism, a totality whose relations follow from the principle of the socialisation of production. Because there is no clear line separating capitalism and socialism, and no necessity producing socialist social relations other than the process and conditions of their construction, the objectives of the socialist movement need to be thought out in detail. It is no use to substitute for evolutionism a radical voluntarism, and for scientism a moralism; social relations have definite conditions of construction and functioning which must be calculated. Only certain social forms *can* be constructed and made durable; the New Jerusalem is not one of them.

Thompson thinks our needs in terms of morality and utopia. Socialism needs principles, and not merely propositions about states of affairs. This is quite true. But it needs principles which can assess and guide the construction of states of affairs, which do not transcend them and merely serve as grounds of criticism in the service of the ideal. It also needs principles which can serve to offer to ordinary people patterns of conduct which they will fight for and attempt to use in their practice. Without such principles we face both opportunism *and* impracticality: political theory and ideology are necessary to any political practice which attempts to transform existing social relations. Principles are necessary not merely as grounds for mobilisation, as moral totem poles, but as a basis of organisation, a means of resolving difficulties and differences, a medium of communication. A non-utopian and non-scientistic socialism may sound like a paradox but that is what we need.

Althusser's work certainly does not offer us the means to think this through. His achievement is of a different order, it arises in large measure from his *failure* to construct the philosophical basis for a new 'orthodoxy', and that is to make the root and branch re-thinking of Marxism a necessity. And that is no mean achievement.

Notes

1 This chapter largely confines itself to the new essay in the collection and does not attempt to consider Thompson's interventions in previous debates – notably the one with Anderson. Where references are made to other essays these are indicated.

I would like to thank Parveen Adams, Mark Cousins and Barry Hindess for their critical comments.

2 There is no more unity to 'Althusserianism' than there was to a previous *bête noire*, 'structuralism'. Many different theories and styles of work are grouped under this catchphrase – some of which I would not hasten to defend. Thompson appears blind to these differences and makes no attempt to survey the work of Althusser's colleagues. If he had considered the works of Lecourt, Fichant, Pêcheux and so on, on epistemology and the history of science, or of Baudelot and Establet on education and on class structure, or of Edelman on law, he would have found it more difficult to present 'Althusserianism' as a closed philosophical ideology spun by the 'Master'. Thompson and others like him like to give the impression that this country has been saturated by 'Althusseriana'. Far from it, most of these important works are ignored or unassimilated. However critical of Althusser *I* may have been, his 'school' remains the most original and productive in modern Marxist theory and research.

3 Thompson here assigns to 'tests' of the consistency of evidence or the validity of propositions relative to evidence an *epistemological function*. These tests are purported to establish the *correspondence* of 'knowledge to properties in the real'. But this 'correspondence' is just what such 'tests' *cannot* establish. This 'correspondence' is a *meta-evidential* question: tests serve to confirm or refute propositions or sift out evidence, they do not validate their own validity but pre-suppose it. Tests require conventions of what counts as evidence, conventions of the adequacy of propositions and procedures to determine it. But those conventions need not make or depend on meta-evidential claims to 'correspondence': garage mechanics are not hot on epistemology but they perform tests according to conventions of evidence and adequacy all the time. The meta-evidential is a level created by the questions of epistemology, it alone raises the problems of 'correspondence' and of the *status* of knowledge relative to it.

4 Thompson comments at this point: 'For a prime example of this misunderstanding, see Hindess and Hirst' (p. 387). No part of *Pre-Capitalist Modes of Production* has attracted more hostile comment and misunderstanding than the Conclusion. In large measure the style of exposition is to blame; it is both excessively polemical and far too condensed. At the same time it must be admitted that the challenge to the idea that historical writing has a primary and special relevance to Marxist social analysis would have been violently rejected, no matter how moderately and carefully expressed. This view we still hold to, and we deplore the extent to which Marxism and social history are virtually equated by large sections of the Left intelligentsia.

Thompson repeats the dominant misunderstanding that we reject the study of the past for the present. As the 'past' is always with us this evidently implies a prohibition on the study of things that 'happened' last week. If the 'past' has no effectivity in the present then the present has no effectivity in the future, etc. We never imagined that these absurdities would parade as criticisms. This is possible only because of our unfortunate play on the word 'past'. We used this word in two senses, one relating to temporality, the other with regard to the effectivity of forms of teleological causality. We must insist that our reference to the ineffectivity of 'past' social relations refers to 'superseded' ones, in the Hegelian sense. This is the *theoretical* position taken in the conclusion, but there will always be readings that refuse to recognise the difference of a *word* and a *concept*, a difference which is even more apparent if concepts are presented in less than rigorous forms.

Our attack on the ineffectivity of the 'past' was a challenge to the Hegelian notion of 'supersession'. In the Hegelian dialectic of development all moments of that dialectic can be co-present, prior moments are superseded (sublated), simultaneously annulled and incorporated in the higher synthesis of the moments which succeed them. From the standpoint of the Absolute the dialectic of development is a single chain, all the parts of which are coincident with each other in the becoming of that which develops. We were concerned to challenge this teleological causality and the spiritual effectivity it entails by introducing a concept of *supersession* in a non-Hegelian sense. This concept of supersession insists that social relations which are replaced by others in a transitional conjuncture become *inexistent* and therefore non-effective. Even in Hegel effectivity implies existence in the form of sublation, a form of existence which is possible because it is *spiritual*. Relations which are existent have effectivity; relations which are superseded by others are replaced in the form of the destructions of their conditions of existence or reproduction. It follows that the study of superseded relations cannot in any sense amount to an analysis of the forms of effectivity of existing relations. History ceases to be a process of *development* in which each of its moments are necessarily linked. Forms of social relations are discontinuous, the transitional conjunctures and the forms of effectivity of social relations do not sum up.

The relevance of this teleological causality may be questioned; surely the Hegelian dialectic has little to do with history? This is not the case, the Hegelian dialectic is the most rigorous form of philosophy of history. Thompson, as we have seen, posits a continuity of historical moments no less complete than Hegel's. Hegel's dialectic explains a *process* but not its end (history is not the development of something, realisation of a given end) – it is to use Althusser's phrase, 'a process without a subject', a process conceivable as itself only by taking the place of the Absolute. It differs from teleological realisations of a given end (Comte, Spencer, etc.) in this rigorous openness, or opaqueness of all but the *form* of its process to knowledge. A philosophy of history is the one rigorous mode of unification or formulation of the object 'history', as a continuous (if not uniform) space of knowledge. It *unifies* this space as possible to be comprehended by a single form of knowledge. This unification is true even of vulgar antiquarian practices in which the 'past' is a given collection of artefacts; such practices treat history as an homogenous field, a continuity in time. If philosophical or antiquarian grounds for the unity of this object are rejected then historical investigations need to base their pertinence on some other claim, for example, current political or ideological relevance. But this introduces radical *discontinuity* into the object, pertinent investigations cease to form an homogenous field. Historical writing, for Marxists, requires conditions other than the historian's practice. At this point Marxist historical writing ceases to find its rationale in a 'discipline', whether historical investigations are pertinent or not becomes a matter of politics. There is no doubt that certain political-ideological arguments are conducted largely or in part in terms of history – the

Russian revolution and its sequel is a case in point. These battles
cannot be avoided on epistemological grounds, they are often a
terrain occupied by the enemy. No one wants to silence leftist and
Marxist historians – the authors of *Pre-Capitalist Modes of
Production* certainly did not – but it is necessary to insist that
historical writing can at best be only one part of Marxist theoretical
and ideological work. That writing must be governed by considerations of its political value and not its contribution to the
'discipline' of history.

Chapter 5

The Uniqueness of the West – Perry Anderson's Analysis of Absolutism and its Problems*

In 1975 Perry Anderson broke the long silence since 'The Components of the National Culture' with a massive two-volume text about the development of the Absolutist state in Europe. In *Lineages of the Absolutist State* Anderson is concerned with the distinct paths of development which characterise Absolutism in Eastern and Western Europe. The first volume, *Passages from Antiquity to Feudalism*, is a preface to the study of Absolutism and treats of the antecedent feudal constitutions which provide the groundwork for Absolutism in different parts of Europe. Two further volumes were promised, the first of them dealing with the major bourgeois revolutions and the second with the structures of the contemporary capitalist states which have emerged from them. Neither has so far appeared.

All in all, this amounts to an attempt to provide a history of the development of and of the variant forms of the state in Europe from Antiquity to the modern period. Anderson insists that this history is confined to the state, it is not a general history and it excludes any specific history of the economic level. Anderson justifies this specific object, the state, on the grounds of its political significance and of its neglect by Marxist historians. It is at the political level that the class struggle is decisively fought out and resolved, and at this level that the relations of production are decisively transformed.

No one would dispute this significance of the state as an object of political theory. The state is only the ostensible object of

*First published in *Economy and Society*, Vol. 4, No. 4, 1975.

Anderson's text, however (at least of the portion of it so far published). Anderson's text *is* about the state, but only in the context of another and wider problem and only in so far as for Anderson the pre-capitalist state is the centre of crystallisation of all social relations. Anderson's history is a general history in the form of a history of the state.

What is the nature of this other problem the form of manifestation of which is the question of the Absolutist state? Why is it that the state is the central and definitive structure of pre-capitalist social relations? The problem which dominates Anderson's text, which governs its major structural feature – the division of feudalism and Absolutism into distinct Eastern and Western European 'trajectories' – is the uniqueness of the West as the locus of the development of capitalism. Only the West produces an autonomous development of capitalism. Anderson seeks this historical confinement of the genesis of capitalism in the unique nature of Western feudalism:

> European feudalism, as we have seen, proved the gateway to
> capitalism. It was the economic dynamic of the feudal mode of
> production in Europe which released the elements of primitive
> accumulation of capital on a continental scale, and it was the
> social order of the Middle Ages which preceded and prepared the
> ascent of the bourgeois class that accomplished it. The full
> capitalist mode of production, launched by the industrial
> revolution, was the gift and malediction of Europe to the globe.
> Today, in the second half of the twentieth century, only one
> region outside of Europe, or its overseas settlements, has
> achieved an advanced industrial capitalism: Japan. (*Lineages*, pp.
> 414–15)

The significance of the state as the primary object of analysis follows from the way in which Anderson defines the general nature of pre-capitalist modes of production in which there are exploitation and classes. Anderson argues that, unlike the capitalist mode of production in which there is a distinct *economic* mechanism of appropriation of the surplus-product, all pre-capitalist modes of production entail the appropriation of the surplus-product through extra-economic sanctions. The various pre-capitalist modes of production are therefore constituted as distinct modes by the particular characteristics of their political and legal superstructures.

The form of the state apparatus is constitutive of the social relations of production, hence the history of the state is a history of pre-capitalist class society *in essence*. The state is a privileged object by reason of Anderson's conception of the social totality.

(i) The problem of the origin

Capitalism comes into existence by 'autonomous' development only in the West. This unique historical origin of capitalism is the result of an antecedent uniqueness. Western feudalism is politically and culturally unlike any other form of 'feudal' society. The parcellisation of sovereignty, the existence of independent towns and the greater freedom of the peasantry which result from this complex and overlapping division of powers, and the legal and cultural forms of European feudalism are features specific to the West and they are loci for the formation of proto-capitalist social forces and social relations. Western European feudalism owes its historical uniqueness to what an old-fashioned Marxist would regard as 'super-structural' features. It is the political-legal constitutions of Western feudalisms which distinguish them from other forms of pre-capitalist landlordship and exploitation of the peasantry through non-economic coercion:

> The original feudal mode of production which triumphed during the early Middle Ages was never simply composed of an elementary set of economic indices, . . . the combination of large-scale agrarian property controlled by an exploiting class, with small-scale production by a tied peasantry, in which surplus labour was pressed out of the latter by *corvées* or dues in kind, was in its generality a very widespread pattern throughout the pre-industrial world. Virtually any post-tribal social formation that did not rest on slavery or nomadism, revealed in this sense forms of landlordism. The singularity of feudalism was never exhausted merely by the existence of seigneurial and serf classes as such. (*Lineages*, p. 408)

Capitalism owes its genesis to a unique historical form, Western feudalism. This form is in turn generated by a unique historical origin. European feudalism originates in a unique 'synthesis' of the civilisation of classical Antiquity, based upon the slave mode of production, with the mode of production and institutions of the

Germanic peoples who conquered the Roman Empire. This 'synthesis' is accomplished in the Dark Ages. From this origin point in Western Europe feudalism radiates out, influencing and developing the proto-feudal social formations of Eastern Europe. These formations were hitherto retarded in their development toward feudalism precisely because of the absence of the creative touchstone of Antiquity.

The existence of a Japanese feudalism merely confirms this uniqueness of the West. For, however similar to Europe it is in structure, Japanese feudalism does not have the same genealogy as Western feudalism. Japanese feudalism did not give rise to an autonomous development of capitalism but to a capitalism induced by the impact of the West. These reflections prompt Anderson to pose a question and to answer it in the following manner:

> What, then, was the specificity of European history, which
> separated it so deeply from Japanese history, despite the common
> cycle of feudalism which otherwise so closely united the two?
> The answer surely lies in the perdurable inheritance of classical
> antiquity. (*Lineages*, p. 420)

Antiquity, the crucial element in the genesis of Western feudalism, is active through this specific feudal constitution in producing a doubly unique historical form, capitalism. It is the *genealogy* of Western feudalism which is the central specific condition of the genesis of capitalism. Capitalism is the product of a unique genesis that stretches back to the Roman world.

Capitalism is not a universal but a unique social form – the specific product of definite and unrepeatable conditions. Because there is a unique origin to capitalism (an origin encapsulated in Antiquity and Western feudalism), the history of its development is a singular and unique *story*. Its reconstruction in a narrative can therefore appear a sufficient account; history through the problem of the origin takes precedence over Marxist theory. This story has a general significance, for the unique pattern of development of the West is nothing less than the development of *history* itself. Capitalism in subordinating the globe to its economic and political relations creates world history and universality. History is the history of the origin and universalisation of capitalism. All other patterns of development exist *as histories* only relative to the history of

capitalism, they exist as evidences of arrested development or
conquered divergence. The unique becomes the universal.

Anderson's text starts from the problem of the unique origin of
Capitalism in the West. It seeks to explain and necessitate this
uniqueness. It attempts to explain the historical specificity of
capitalism by ascribing to it and reconstructing for it a unique
genealogy. A genealogy must therefore be discovered which
explains the uniqueness of its outcome, why capitalism appears
where it does and nowhere else. The genealogy must itself be
unique in order to explain the uniqueness of its outcome. This
uniqueness of the genealogy is founded on the singular and
unrepeatable circumstances of *its* origin. The uniqueness of the
origin point of capitalism is explained by the uniqueness of its
origin in turn.

Anderson's problem and the history it generates is a teleological
one. The problem of uniqueness requires that capitalism be
conceived as the definite *end* of a history. Capitalism is conceived as
an *end* because its uniqueness is explained as the outcome of a
particular and unrepeatable history. Its uniqueness is made
necessary, made unique, by the singularity of the history which is its
origin. History is therefore written with its end (capitalism) as the
object to be explained. It is the constitution of this object *as an end*
(the outcome of a unique history) which is the mode in which it is
explained. Capitalism becomes necessarily unique (and is therefore
explained) by being the end of a history, it is the end of *this* history
and no other. As the end is conceived of as unique the necessitation
of its uniqueness must be at the level of the unique too, the
uniqueness of the end requires a unique origin.

To seek to explain the uniqueness of an historical form or
phenomenon necessarily entails the problem of the origin. It is only
in the singularity of the origin that uniqueness becomes conceivable
and necessary. Uniqueness must be conceived as an end and the end
ascribed to an origin. This teleology is inherent in the problem of
uniqueness. Posing uniqueness as a *problem* pre-supposes the
explanation of the uniqueness in the origin, it is a question of the
problematic of the origin. The answer is prior to the question,
necessary for it to be posed.

Capitalism is not the end of *all* history. Anderson is not
concerned to construct a universal teleology; a philosophy of
history in which history is the finite process of realisation of a single

end. Capitalism is the end of history in so far as it is the object of his explanation. Its necessitation as a unique object requires the connection origin → end. It is *an* end because it is necessitated by genealogy, by development from an origin. It is not the only conceivable end. That history does not end for Anderson with the genesis of capitalism is not at issue. It is his method of investigation which is teleological, it converts the object to be explained into an end. Capitalism is conceived as the end of a genealogy; conceived as an end *because* a genealogy, a specific origin, is sought for it. Anderson is committed to defining his object teleologically because of the question he has asked: why is capitalism unique to the West?

Anderson avoids a teleological explanation of his teleologically defined object. He avoids attributing this genealogy to some necessitating cause. Capitalism is necessitated as a unique object by its genealogy, by its unique origin, but that origin is not necessitated, nor is the pattern for development from the origin. Anderson avoids a full-blown philosophy of history. This refusal of teleological explanation is a function of Anderson's commitment to 'empirical' history.[1] His method of proving that the origin is unique is to attempt to demonstrate that it has not existed elsewhere – in other words the 'comparative method' is a central element of proof in Anderson's work. D. G. MacRae in a short review was correct to draw attention to the centrality of this method to Anderson's text and to note its distance from Marxism.[2] This so-called 'method' is nothing but speculative empiricism. The presence of a certain outcome or characteristic in a given case is attributed more or less plausibly to certain given features which the case in question possesses and other chosen cases lack. There is no way in which the causal efficacy of the attributed features can be proven or the process of speculative comparison terminated. Other, unknown, features may in fact be the ones efficacious in the case. Comparison cannot be limited since we have no notion of what it is that is being compared, the range of comparison can only be terminated arbitrarily. In his use of this 'method' Anderson resembles another investigator concerned to explain the 'uniqueness' of Western capitalism, Max Weber.

Given the refusal of a philosophy of history Anderson is condemned to the comparative method – uniqueness is attributed to the West by reason of the absence of similar characteristics or potentialities in other regions. The uniqueness of the West therefore becomes the uniqueness of a narrative – the necessity of the unique is founded on the singularity of its genealogy. Because he refuses teleological *explanation* Anderson must found uniqueness on the singularity of an *event*, an origin no other evolution can share. The conditional necessity of genealogy becomes necessity only in so far as the uniqueness of the origin can be defended by the comparative method. The problem Anderson poses, the uniqueness of the West, requires either a philosophy of history, or a speculative empiricism as its method of explanation.

Ultimately, the uniqueness of a genealogy if it is to be grounded against contingency and 'empirical' refutation must be grounded on an essence, that is, a non-conditional existence which contains within itself the possibility of all subsequent development. It is for this reason that the only rigorous philosophies of history are *idealist* ones. Only the *spiritual* is non-conditional. Anderson avoids this rigorous idealism. This is not entirely to his credit. What is it that is so singular about Antiquity that it qualifies as the *origin*? Speculative empiricism cannot tell us. It can only attribute causal efficacy to given features by their absence in other cases, it cannot explain causation without comparison. The function of speculative empiricism is to *isolate* the origin, it cannot explain why it is the origin. On the specific contribution of Antiquity, that which qualifies it as vital to an autonomous capitalism, Anderson is extremely vague. The chapter on the nature of the 'synthesis' is one of the briefest and most inconclusive in the whole text. Far from explaining *what* is 'synthesised', why Antiquity is crucial in the formation of Western feudalism, Anderson devotes the bulk of the chapter to the role of the Church as 'the indispensable bridge between the two epochs' (*Passages*, p. 137) and a description of the Carolingian Constitution. Since Anderson does not argue that elements of the slave mode of production or of classical techniques of production are central in the legacy of Antiquity, or that elements of the imperial polity are of special importance, this legacy can only be *legal* and *cultural*. Roman law and the Christian religious ideology are the most substantial residues of the decline of the Ancient World. Does Anderson intend to attribute to these cultural forms the decisive role in the genealogy of capitalism? There can be no answer, for the precise significance of Antiquity is never defined. Anderson's vast exercise in speculative empiricism rests on a profound ambiguity. This silence, at the very centre of his thesis, is a necessary one – it is this silence which spares him from a complete collapse into idealism.

It is Anderson's *problem* which is teleological. The question of the *uniqueness* of Western capitalism is not a necessary or inevitable one. Anderson evidently conceives the alternative to his position and his problem to be some form of evolutionism. Anderson justifies the problem of uniqueness thus:

> But what rendered the unique passage to capitalism possible in Europe was *the concatenation of antiquity and feudalism*. In other words to grasp the secret of the emergence of the capitalist mode of production in Europe, it is necessary to discard in the most radical way possible any conception of it as simply an evolutionary subsumption of a lower mode of production by a higher mode of production, the one generated automatically and entirely from within the other by an organic internal succession, and therewith effacing it. (*Lineages*, p. 420)

Genealogy as unique development and evolutionism are not the exclusive and opposed conceptions of history. It is not necessary in opposing Anderson's thesis to be committed to some form of teleological and unilinear evolutionism.

Anderson is, as we have seen, committed by the very problem he poses to necessitating the development of capitalism in the West as a unique and exclusive development. This development is essential to the West and singular because of the unrepeatable circumstances of its origin. Anderson is logically committed to a thesis which he never explicitly states – that without the specific circumstances of the origin from which capitalism develops in the West there could be no capitalism as we know it. The very thesis of uniqueness attempts to make the West the exclusive source of capitalism. The possibility of autonomous Japanese development is challenged.

The fact that capitalism developed in Western Europe between the fifteenth and the eighteenth centuries proves nothing about its potentialities for autonomous development elsewhere. The 'West' is not a unique origin point but simply the site of the first and successful conjuncture of transition to capitalism. The effects of this transition have been to destroy the possibility of other 'autonomous' transitions. Western capitalism is dominant in the process of transition to capitalism, it subordinates and overcomes other modes of production through the development of the world market and imperialism. The successful resolution of a transitional conjuncture in the form of the development of capitalism, whatever its spatio-temporal location, must result in the subordination of precapitalist modes at a more or less rapid pace, and with this process of subordination the closure of the possibility of all other conjunctures of transition toward capitalism. Japanese or Russian feudal forms may or may not have generated the conditions necessary for a transitional conjuncture (given, that is, the conditions of an autonomous development). There is no way of knowing since the existence of a successful transitional conjuncture has closed all such possibilities of development. This closure does not justify the notion that the West is 'unique'. *There is no essential historical process* – whether it be the necessary evolutionary progress of all social forms through a succession of 'stages', or, the unique and unrepeatable confinement of a development to a distinct origin. The question of uniqueness answers itself once we have shed the essentialist problem of the origin, these countries in Western Europe happen to be dominant in the first and successful transition to capitalism.

To ask the question – why is it that capitalism develops *first* in the West? – is to pose a question not asked by Anderson. Indeed, his problematic excludes it, the possibility of capitalism is confined to Western feudalism. Feudalism originates in a unique and nowhere repeatable 'synthesis' of Antiquity and the Germanic peoples. Other autonomous capitalisms are denied in principle. The sole form of non-European feudalism accepted by Anderson, that of Japan, is argued to depend for the conditions of transition on the impact of the West and to lack the possibility of the Western dynamic because of the absence of the legacy of Antiquity.

The question of priority leads, however, to an equally essentialistic and teleological definition of an object of investigation. Again the mode of proof of the necessity of priority must be some form of speculative empiricism or an idealism. The problems of the uniqueness or of the priority of the development of capitalism to the West are non-problems for, or rather they should be non-problems for, Marxism. This is not because Marxism is an evolutionism but because, on the contrary, in so far as Marxism is not a philosophy of history or a comparative sociology, there can be for it no necessary form of historical process.

Evolutionism and genealogy both involve an historical process with a definite and necessary form. For evolutionism history is a unity because of the universality of the action of the cause of evolutionary progress and of the inevitability of the succession of 'stages' consequent upon the action of that cause. For genealogy a history is a unique pattern of development made possible by the singularity of its origin – this pattern is necessarily unique but not inevitable. Genealogy derives the essentiality of its history from a unique origin and evolutionism the necessity of its history from a universally acting cause. They differ in the form in which they create an essential pattern of development, but not in their theoretical consequences for Marxism. The theoretical effect of the problem of 'uniqueness' is the displacement of Marxist theoretical concepts and their replacement by the speculative empiricism of the comparative method.

(ii) Marxist theory and speculative empiricism

We will now consider Anderson's relation to Marxist theoretical concepts, registering the effects of this displacement. Anderson's problem leads him to a speculative empiricist reconstruction of the *trajectory* of European feudalism. He is concerned to show how it is only in the West that the conditions of autonomous transition are produced by separating European feudalism into Eastern and Western zones with distinct 'trajectories'. He produces an historical narrative, telling distinct sets of stories called 'trajectories', and this narrative is underpinned by comparisons which attempt to show the stories are distinct. Anderson adopts an historian's practice which necessitates the displacement of Marxist theory. Marxist concepts do not organise and conduct the analysis, they are at best secondary to so-called 'empirical' history. Nine-tenths of Anderson's text consists of narratives of the features of the state in particular regions and countries. *Lineages*, for example, consists of chapters on Spain, France, England, Italy, Sweden, Poland, Prussia, Austria, Russia and the Ottoman Empire. These narratives settle nothing, nor do the comparative generalisations that are supposed to be based on them.

Anderson makes no attempt to start from Marxist theoretical concepts in the definition of the problems of investigation, to use them as means of analysis, or as proofs of the analysis. For example, the *concept* of *mode of production* plays no active function in analysis. Anderson does not start with a specification of the concept, with a theoretical delineation of the concepts of specific modes of production, nor does he attempt to demonstrate that the specific social formations he considers are or are not dominated by a particular mode. For Anderson the form of the state is constitutive of the social relations of production, hence modes of production are identified with and by differences in state constitution as revealed in 'empirical' history. There is no need for concepts of the various modes, or of conceptual criteria of proof (to show, for example, that an analysis is not merely confused or that conceptual confusion has the effect of creating 'modes of production' through failure to separate distinct conceptual elements). Modes of production are identified by the empirical isolation of significant differences in state constitution, the structure of the mode will follow from the 'given' institutions encountered. This displaces one of the most central general concepts in Marxist theory and replaces it by the results of 'empirical' history.

In Anderson's text questions of Marxist theory have the status of being dependent on generalisations from the historian's narrative or of reflections ancillary to this narrative. It is the form of the narrative and the 'conclusions' derived from the speculative empiricist practice which operates on it which decide the fate of Marxist theoretical concepts. Anderson makes no attempt to provide rigorous *theoretical* arguments or conceptual proofs for the positions he advances about Marxist theory.

We have argued that the problem of 'uniqueness' is not a Marxist problem and that it must displace the questions and concepts of Marxist theory. Theory is displaced from its organising role by the dominance of narrative (the means through which the genealogy is reconstructed) and speculative comparison (in which the uniqueness of the genealogy is 'proved'). Anderson's text *must* turn into a series of narratives and comparisons. The problem of the origin explains uniqueness through the singularity of its genealogy. The unique is the conclusion of an unrepeatable *story*. Narrative is the explanatory form for this problematic – the construction of a genealogy and its defence by proving its singularity by comparison with other patterns of development. Given Anderson's problem the dominance of narrative is a necessary *theoretical* effect.

Anderson makes no attempt to theoretically reflect on this practice or to state its relation to Marxist theory. There is no attempt to state the consequences of this adoption of a non-Marxist problem ('uniqueness') and method (comparison). Anderson merely challenges evolutionalism. He is in particular silent about Althusser and Balibar's attempt to construct a non-evolutionist and non-empiricist Marxist theory of history. Can it be that Anderson believes his narrative is its own proof; that the proof of his practice is at the level of the 'empirical', to be confirmed or disconfirmed by the analogous practices of other historians? If so he would be mistaken. The question he has asked is not an 'empirical' one, nor is the mode of analysis it inspires 'empirical'. Anderson's work raises theoretical questions even if it does not argue them.

An example of Anderson's practice in relation to Marxist theory is the question of the role of genesis structure in the concept of mode of production. Anderson notes that in the *Grundrisse* Marx argues that the genesis of a mode of production must be distinguished from its structure. Anderson uses this distinction to contend that although Japanese feudalism had a similar structure to the West it had a different *genesis*. It is this genesis which is decisive in explaining the different consequences of feudalism in Japan and the West:

> The whole genealogy of feudalism in Japan . . . presents an
> unequivocal contrast with the descent of feudalism in Europe . . .
> Against the background of this radical diversity of origins, the
> *structural* similarity of European and Japanese feudalism is only
> the more striking: the most eloquent demonstration of all that a
> mode of production, once constituted, reproduces its own
> rigorous unity as an integrated system, 'clear' of the disparate
> presuppositions which initially gave birth to it. . . . Yet, having
> stressed the fundamental parallelism between European and
> Japanese feudalism, as internally articulated modes of pro-
> duction, there remains the simple, enormous fact of their
> divergent outcome. (*Lineages*, pp. 418–19)

Anderson remarks that Marx was wrong to assume that the constituted structure of a mode of production obliterates the conditions of its genesis. This commits Anderson to arguing that the conditions of genesis of the structure are effective independently of it and have a decisive influence on it. Anderson illustrates this with a striking passage:

The 'advantage' of Europe over Japan lay in its classic ante-
cedence, which even after the Dark Ages did not disappear
'behind' it, but survived in certain basic respects 'in front' of it. In
this sense, the concrete historical genesis of feudalism in Europe,
far from vanishing like fire and vapour into the terrestrial solidity
of the accomplished structure, had tangible effects on its final
dissolution. (*Lineages*, p. 421)

Logically, it is the specific non-structural conditions of the genesis
of modes of production which are decisive in historical causation –
genesis dominates structure and reproduces its effects through it.

Anderson argues for the decisive role of the origin because
'concrete *social formations* . . . typically embody a number of
coexistent and conflicting modes of production of varying date'
(*Lineages*, p. 421). It is the historical combination of modes, a
specific circumstance subject to no general causes, which determines the specific paths of development. This is nothing but special
pleading for the privilege of genesis, for a privilege which
vouchsafes Anderson's problem the status of a Marxist problem. It
can appear to be an argument only because Anderson fails to raise
the *theoretical* status of combinations. For the Marxist theory of
modes of production the combination of modes raises the question
of the *form* of that combination – under what conditions is it
possible for distinct modes to combine, what is the articulation of
the combination and the form of reproduction of the combination?
In the absence of a rigorous general concept of mode of production
and of concepts of at least certain specific modes this question
cannot be posed or investigated theoretically. This question is an
impossible one for Anderson since he rejects any attempt to
construct *concepts* of determinate modes of production – modes
are defined by the empirical form of the state and empirical
differences in superstructural constitution. Combination must also
be an 'empirical' question, modes of production will form any
particular 'coexistent and conflicting' mixture that he happens to
discover.

Combination is itself a structure and not a happenstance. The
theoretical question of the *form* of combination raises the problems
of correspondence, articulation and dominance. Distinct modes of
production cannot form a simple co-existent and co-present unity
since each of them supposes a definite mechanism of appropriation

of the surplus product, definite class relations[3] and political conditions of class rule. How would it be possible for the conditions of reproduction of each of the modes to be secured in parallel to and independently of the others? Combination presupposes definite articulations of the modes at the political and economic level. *Combinations in dominance*, in which one mode of production subordinates the conditions of reproduction of the other mode/modes combined with it, and where one ruling class is dominant in the class alliance and struggle which must characterise the complex state form of the combination, is the general form of the combination of modes of production. As a definite structure, which takes the form of articulation *as* dominance, the combination is not reducible to the conjuncture of its formation, its development and effects are not independent of this articulation.

Combination is both conjunctural and structured. Since combination is the formation of a structure Anderson has not overcome the genesis/structure problem by reference to the complexity of social formations. Logically the combination of elements into a mode and the combination of modes into a complex structure are not different. The conditions of *genesis* could only be the decisive factor Anderson supposes them to be if they are effective independently of the structure formed from them. Thus Anderson ascribes the difference of European and Japanese feudalism to the circumstances of their *origin* – he does not argue that it is because they form different complex structures of combination. Indeed, for all the talk of complexity, Anderson treats medieval Europe and Tokugawa Japan as in effect single homogeneous structures of social relations and not as combinations. The 'synthesis' of Antiquity and Germanic society is not a *combination*, it does not combine modes but fuses them into a single new mode – what is synthesised is left in doubt. It is not the different structures of combination of modes of production that lead to the respective outcomes in Japan and Europe, it is the conditions antecedent to the formation of a single mode of production, the feudal mode. Those conditions are in fact predominantly cultural.

Anderson is committed by his mode of explanation of the uniqueness of the West to the position that it is the non-structural particular conditions of the genesis of a mode of production which are dominant over the structure of the mode itself, and that the combination of modes is not itself a structure, its form is a function of circumstances. This abolishes the space for *any* attempt to construct a general concept of the social totality and to assign a definite causal efficacy to the elements of its structure. It is the non-structural historically unique conditions of the formation of a structure which are the determinant of its consequences and effects. This radical inversion of genesis and structure subordinates the theory of the social totality to the 'discoveries' of history – social causation is inexplicable except by reference to the origin.

Anderson conceives his position to be opposed to historicism, he claims to have broken with 'any purely linear notion of historical time as a whole' (*Lineages*, p. 421). Lineality appears to consist in some form of evolutionism, 'a cumulative chronology in which one phase succeeds and supersedes the next, to produce a successor that will surpass it' (*Lineages*, p. 421). Anderson appears to conflate historicism and evolutionism, lineality is the succession of stages from lower to higher in a continuous and uninterrupted development. Far from having broken with linear time or historicism Anderson's position merely represents another variant of it. 'Historical time as a whole' is formally beyond Anderson's compass, but his study concerns a finite unity of development which is complete as a history. Lineality permits of the reversals and delayed effects Anderson argues mark him off from evolutionism. Lineality pertains to the unity of the process, to its definition by its end. It is the process of development of that end. Anderson's history is an 'envelope' of time and development sealed by the uniqueness of the origin. The unity of Anderson's history is the unity of development from the origin and the confinement of that development to this origin. This unique and privileged development is the measure of all other historical times related to it or which intersect with it. The development of the West is the time against which other developments are backward or divergent. The West is privileged, is the time of times, because it is the locus of development of the end which is the object of Anderson's history.

Anderson's position is, despite his protests, historicist. Anderson's rejection of historicism is a gesture, a gesture toward a position he never confronts. Anderson fails to discuss and to challenge the positions of Althusser and Balibar in *Reading Capital* which, whatever their defects, present a thoroughgoing critique of historicism, a critique which includes the type of geneticism Anderson proposes. There is a massive discrepancy between the serious and meticulous regard for the texts and the disputes of historians and the massive silence with respect to Marxist theory. This silence and this gesture call to mind others. His silence corresponds to his failure to produce an answer to the points made in Poulantzas's critical text. Anderson's response was a displaced and gestural one, the attempt to incorporate 'structuralist' concepts into his 'Components of the National Culture'.[4]

(iii) The concept of mode of production

In the main body of his text Anderson uses no clear or coherent concept of mode of production; his usage is ad hoc, shifting and contradictory. The elements which appear to be characteristic of a mode of production vary in different sections of the text. Thus the slave mode of production appears to be constituted by the presence and use of a particular status of labourer, the slave. Anderson confines his discussion of this mode to the extent to which slaves were used and to the role of slavery in retarding the development of the forces of production in Antiquity. What the slave modes' forces of production *are* is never considered and certainly never conceptualised, nor is there any attempt to essay its relations of production. The feudal mode of production is conceived as an historically specific complex of institutions – legal and political forms. Decisive in this complex is the vassallage – fief system and the dispersal of state power which results from it: 'this parcellisation of sovereignty was constitutive of the whole feudal mode of production' (*Passages*, p. 148). In the case of the 'nomadic' mode of production it is a definite production technique – a certain regime of pastoralism – which is constitutive. Thus a mode of production may be defined variously by the socio-legal status of the labourer, by the form of division of state power, and by a set of technical conditions of production. Modes of production may be constituted at the level of the legal form of the relations of production, the level of the political superstructure or at the level of production technique. Any level of the structure-superstructure couple may be the determinant in constituting a mode of production it appears. None of these usages is argued for or defended theoretically.

In the conclusion of *Lineages* Anderson proposes another form of conceiving pre-capitalist modes of production which confines the determination of the characteristics of modes to one definite level.

This conception, far from solving the difficulties which stem from the incoherence in the body of the text, destroys the concept mode of *production* in any recognisable Marxist sense.

Anderson ushers in this remarkable conception through a critique of the orthodox Marxist concept of the feudal mode of production. In orthodox Marxism the feudal mode is primarily defined by the form of appropriation of the surplus product, *feudal rent*, and feudal relations of production are compatible with a number of variant forms of legal and political constitution. Anderson criticises this conception in the following manner:

> All privilege to Western development is thereby held to disappear. . . . Feudalism, in this version of materialist historiography, becomes an absolving ocean in which virtually any society may receive its baptism. The scientific invalidity of this theoretical ecumenicism can be demonstrated from the logical paradox in which it results. For if, in effect, the feudal mode of production can be defined independently of the variant juridical and political superstructures which accompany it . . . the problem then arises: how is the unique dynamism of the European theatre of international feudalism to be explained? (*Lineages*, p. 402)

The effect of this orthodox Marxist reduction of feudalism to a simple economic nexus is that the determinants of the differential development of the West must be sought in what is specific to it, that is, at the level of the superstructure:

> Laws and states, dismissed as secondary and insubstantial, re-emerge with a vengeance as the apparent authors of the most momentous break in modern history . . . once the whole structure of sovereignty and legality is *dissociated* from the economy of universal feudalism, its shadow paradoxically governs the world: for it becomes the only principle capable of explaining the essential development of the whole (. . . capitalist . . .) mode of production. (*Lineages*, p. 403)

Thus materialism is turned into idealism.

This critique depends for its force on the reader accepting a premise and failing to notice a consequence. It depends on our accepting that the problem of the uniqueness of the West is a valid problem. It further assumes that Marxists are going to attempt to solve this problem by means of Anderson's speculative empiricist method and in doing so attribute the differential outcome to the same features present in the West and absent elsewhere as Anderson does. This problem of the uniqueness of the West is not a Marxist problem; the Marxist has only to answer that the problem of other transitions is impossible and the problem of 'uniqueness' is a Weberian illusion to remove the central condition of Anderson's critique. Assume a Marxist attempts to answer another question (which, as we have seen, Anderson does not ask), that of *priority* of the West. This may be answered not at the level of the superstructure but at the level of the economy – for example, in terms of the more rapid development of the forces of production due to natural advantages, the impact of the discovery of America and the stimulus of the influx of precious metals. Indeed, the question of 'uniqueness' may be answered at this level too. Whether or not these explanations are good ones is not at issue here, the point is that there is no necessity of attributing the different outcomes to political and legal forms. Hence the couple ecumenicism-idealism does not logically follow – it only follows if one attempts to answer Anderson's problem in Anderson's manner.

Having criticised the conventional Marxist conception of feudalism for resulting in 'a perverse idealism', Anderson manages to fail to notice that he makes this very idealism (no longer perverse because it is systematic) the constitutive basis of all pre-capitalist modes of production in which there is exploitation. Anderson proposes to differentiate modes of production by variations in the form of their superstructures. The effect of this is to reduce the relations of production to political-legal constitutions. It appears that the conventional Marxist conception is at fault in falling into a paradox – of materialist premises that lead to idealist explanations. Idealism without paradox is permissible.

Anderson proposes this remarkable conception of mode of production as a *solution* to the contradiction he identifies as the consequence of the classic 'economistic' Marxist concept of mode of production. Anderson argues that:

> The solution of this paradox lies . . . in the very definition given by Marx of pre-capitalist social formations. *All* modes of production in class societies prior to capitalism extract surplus labour from the immediate producers by means of extra-economic coercion. Capitalism is the first mode of production in

history in which the means whereby the surplus is pumped out of
the direct producer is 'purely' economic in form. . . . All other
previous modes of exploitation operate through *extra-economic*
sanctions – kin, customary, religious, legal or political. It is
therefore on principle always impossible to read them off from
economic relations as such. (*Lineages*, p. 403)

Note the phrase 'economic relations as such'. What is the nature of
these relations *as such*? Clearly, they can be nothing more than
forms of production technique. The relations of production are
excluded from 'economic relations as such'. Anderson follows on
with this amazing passage:

The superstructures of kinship, religion, laws or the state
necessarily enter into the constitutive structure of the mode of
production in pre-capitalist social formations. They intervene
directly in the 'internal' means of surplus-extraction, where in
capitalist social formations, the first in history to separate the
economy as a formally self-contained order, they provide by
contrast its 'external' preconditions. (*Lineages*, pp. 403–4)

In defining the precise form of extra-economic *sanction* the
superstructure is constitutive of the mode of appropriation of the
surplus product and, therefore, of the relations of production. The
conclusion which follows from this is predictable:

In consequence, pre-capitalist modes of production cannot be
defined *except* via their political legal and ideological superstructures, since these are what determine the type of extra-economic
coercion that specifies them. (*Lineages*, p. 404)

Pre-capitalist modes of production are differentiated by the type of
sanction employed, these sanctions are *determined* in type by the
form of the superstructure. The superstructure is in effect constitutive of the whole mode of production.

The 'economic . . . as such' is given independently of the
superstructure in certain socio-technical conditions of production
which we may presume the direct producers already possess.
Imposed upon these conditions is a form of extra-economic
exploitation, the nature of this exploitation and of the exploiting
class is defined by the precise legal, ideological and political
constitution of the state from which the sanctions derive. How are

modes of production to be specified? By the form of the superstructure. *This means that there can be as many modes of production as there are distinct legal-political constitutions and forms of extra-economic sanction which follow from them.* Modes of production may be defined purely at the level of the superstructure and without reference to the specific structure of production – all that is required to designate a mode is a special form of sanction.

The different types of political constitution and form of sanction are simply given. Anderson makes no attempt to explain the conditions of existence of these variant state forms, they are merely products of historical circumstances. No wonder Anderson is committed to the primacy of genesis over structure. It is only through the historical circumstances of its genesis, the given political forms present in the case, that a mode of production acquires definite characteristics. The effect of Anderson's position is to dissolve modes of production as definite economic structures – modes of production are reduced to forms of exploitation. A pre-capitalist mode of production is for Anderson the simple combination of a particular historically formed polity with some given set of conditions of production possessed by the direct producers independently of that polity.

In what sense are these 'modes' envisaged by Anderson modes *of production*? The theoretical effects of his position are to reduce the social relations of production to the superstructure (to ideological–juridical forms and to sanctions) and to reduce the forces of production to a set of socio-technical conditions of production which have no necessary connection with the mode of appropriation of the surplus product. Production as a system of social relations is left untheorised, it is a given external to the constitutive element of a mode of production, the form of the state. The nature of the relation of the forces and means of production to the form of appropriation of the surplus product does not merit one line of general theoretical reflection in Anderson's text. What given forms of production are compatible with specific historical forms of state is an 'empirical' matter.

The classic Marxist concept of mode of production, a concept designated in *Capital*, is a combination of the forces and relations of production; these forms are combined as the structure of social relations of the economy. The mode of appropriation of the surplus product is necessarily connected with a definite social form of production. The social relations of production produce a definite distribution of the means of production, this distribution constitutes the form of division of the product into necessary and surplus labour, this distribution and this division designates the agents socially necessary to production. The relations of production constitute the mode of appropriation of the surplus product and the social division of labour. The social conditions of existence of production structure the form of the forces of production (the 'technical' division of labour and forms of organisation of the labour process – these are *social* relations and not simply technique). Marxism conceives the relations of production as the dominant aspect of the *economic structures* – they are part of the economic structure and in a definite combination with the forces of production they constitute that structure. Hence there is no simple correspondence of forces and relations of production as given entities prior to and external to one another; the forces of production derive their specific character as the forces of a particular mode of production from their articulation and combination with the relations of production. It follows that a mode of production must have a definite structure of the forces of production specific to it, an effect of its articulation-combination with the production relations. Anderson's position clearly implies the opposite.

Anderson's position displaces this articulation-combination. As a result the relation of the forces of production to the conditions of appropriation of the surplus product is untheorised. The difference between the superstructure and the social relations of production is never posed as a theoretical question. Anderson remarks that capitalist social formations are 'the first in history to separate the economy as a *formally* self-contained order'; either, this means nothing more than capitalism requires the creation of a 'private' sphere through its juridical categories, a necessary form for free capital and free wage labour, or, it means that only capitalism has an *economic structure* in the strict sense – that there is no distinct set of social relations of production in non-capitalist modes, that these relations are fused into the superstructure. The Marxist concept of mode of production is a *general* concept – this is certainly the position of the '1859 Preface' and the '1857 Introduction'. Anderson wants to confine it to the capitalist mode of production. One might suggest that Anderson as a Marxist theorist, having proposed a radical transformation of the concept mode of production, might have taken these questions we have raised seriously or at least posed them. Marxism is not a dogma, as a scientific theory it must undergo a constant process of criticism and theoretical development. However, if Anderson's practice were to become the norm central theoretical concepts would be discarded without serious theoretical analysis or argument.

Perhaps Anderson feels that this is unnecessary, that he has Marx's 'authority' for this radical revision. He cites Marx when he says that pre-capitalist modes depend on extra-economic coercion to extract the surplus product, this apparently justifies his conclusion that such modes 'cannot be defined *except* via their . . . superstructures'. This means that such modes can *only* be differentiated at this level. Marx conceives the differentiation of modes of production very differently in *Capital*:

> The essential difference between the various economic forms of
> society, between, for instance, a society based on slave-labour,
> and one based on wage labour, lies only in the mode in which this
> surplus labour is in each case extracted from the actual producer,
> the labourer. (*Capital* 1: 217)

Marx here defines modes of production at the level of the social relations of production, in terms of the *mode* of appropriation of the surplus product, and not at the level of the superstructural conditions of that mode. It is the economic form of exploitation and not the sanctions which support it that is the means of differentiation. Marx's position is that the social relations of production and the superstructure are not fused or equivalent. The political and ideological conditions of existence of exploitation are not exploitation itself, legal forms of expression of property relations are not the actual economic relations of possession and control.

The difference of the superstructure and the relations of production admits of the possibility of discrepancy between them. The possibility of difference and variation between the relations of production and the forms of political constitution is in effect denied by Anderson. For those Marxists who have argued that feudal state power might take variant forms while being based upon the basic feudal production relation, feudal rent, are contending no more than this, and they are clearly operating within the limits of the

Marxist concept of social totality. Anderson is hardly going to deny that capitalist relations of production are compatible with various forms of political constitution – constitutional monarchies, democratic republics, fascist dictatorships, Bonapartist regimes, etc. Why are all these forms compatible with capitalism? – because the social relations of production are untouched by this variance. Anderson finds it inconceivable that feudal social relations might exhibit a similar constancy. *The reason for attacking the orthodox conception of feudalism is that it denies the uniqueness of the West. Anderson is led into arguing for the superstructural determination of pre-capitalist modes of production to save his own problem as a Marxist problem.*

The actual reason Anderson advances for superstructural determination is that pre-capitalist modes depend upon non-economic coercion to extract the surplus product. Marx does take this position but he never says that the form of appropriation of the surplus product differs simply with the variation in the form of sanction which backs it – that exploitation through pre-capitalist rent differs in *form* because a monastery or a feudal baron or a non-noble landlord without seignorial power extracts it. The *form* of appropriation remains the same, it is the level of coercion or its efficiency which varies in these cases. It is the economic form of appropriation (through rent, slave labour, etc.) which constitutes the basis of the production and not the extra-economic coercion which supports it. It is this form which is articulated with definite forces of production.

Marx differentiates (in so far as he attempted to do so) forms of exploitation of the surplus product and not forms of extra-economic sanction. For Anderson the two must be equivalent. The *forms* of exploitation (e.g., feudal rent, etc.) do provide the means of designating the complex unity of forces and relations of production constitutive of a mode. Anderson's position, however, provides no limit to the possibility of constructing 'modes of production' (which have nothing to do with *production*). Take some given technical form of production (which need not be specified except to indicate that it is non-capitalist), add extra-economic coercion, and the result is quite logically that exploitation by political 'bosses', bandits, warlords, etc., provides the basis of constituting distinct modes of production. Is not banditry a distinct form of coercion, and is it not a form of exploitation of the direct producers? Then, if we apply Anderson's conception logically, do we not have a new mode of production, the 'bandit mode of production'?

Marx's position in *Capital* on pre-capitalist modes of production does entail definite difficulties; these difficulties centre on the question of the non-economic nature of coercion. Anderson's solution to these difficulties is not to see them, to reduce the forms of exploitation to coercion and the relations of production to the superstructure. In Marx's formulations there is a profound ambiguity about the status of the non-economic forms of coercion – his conception of pre-capitalist forms must be problematised and its difficulties resolved by means of Marxist concepts. Anderson does not do this. He takes what is problematical (the status of coercion) as the solution to a problem (a 'problem', we should add, that he has created).

Before we proceed let us be clear about the status of the positions of Marx which are in question. We are not dealing with a systematic attempt to construct concepts of pre-capitalist modes of production, but with incidental remarks and brief passages in discourses devoted to other objects. The section of the *Grundrisse*, 'Pre-Capitalist Economic Formations', is not concerned with producing a theory of pre-capitalist modes of production, it is an account of genealogy of the categories pre-supposed in capitalism – capital and free labour. Modes of production are touched on only incidentally, the central object of the text is the form of appearance of the conditions of labour and possession/property to the economic subjects in the different pre-capitalist forms. Similarly, in *Capital* Marx uses the differentiation capitalism/pre-capitalism to illustrate forms he considers unique to capitalism; pre-capitalist forms are not the object of theorisation. This is particularly the case in Chapter XLVII of *Capital* on pre-capitalist forms of ground rent. The function of the chapter is not to investigate these forms but to illustrate the specificity of capitalist ground rent – to show that rent is not the form of appropriation of the surplus product under capitalism.

Capital employs a relatively simple differentiation of capitalism and pre-capitalist forms: this is as follows: (i) capitalism = the separation of the direct producer from the means of production, the subsumption of the direct producer in a process of production structured by exploitative relations of production, and the consequent dominance of the economic instance; (ii) pre-capitalist forms = the non-separation of the direct producer from the means of production, the consequent necessity of a non-economic form to secure and sanction the relations of exploitation, and the consequent dominance of a non-economic instance in the social formation. This position leads Marx to the conclusion:

> [I]n all forms in which the direct producer remains the 'possessor' of the means of production . . . the property relationship must simultaneously appear as a direct relation of lordship and servitude, so that the direct producer is not free. . . . Under such conditions the surplus-labour for the nominal owner of the land can only be extorted from them by other than economic pressure, whatever the form assumed may be. (*Capital* III: 771)

Here is the problem which allows Anderson his solution. Relations of production *appear* as relations of dominance and rest on extra-economic coercion. Anderson makes the appearance the reality and fails to see Marx's position as the site of a problem. Anderson is satisfied to equate social relations of production and domination since it serves his purposes to do so. The effect of this position is, as we have seen, the dissolution of the general concept of mode of production as an articulated combination of forces and relations of production.

Marx's difficulty does not require or legitimate this solution since Marxist theory itself provides us with the concepts to overcome it. The concepts of the *forms* of appropriation of the surplus product provide an initial and elementary means of division of the relations of production and the superstructure as we have seen. Further, the notion of the 'possession' of the means of production by the labourer and of the separation of the exploiter from control of these means must be problematised. Anderson forgets that categories like 'possession' have to be *conceptualised* for each mode of production – they are not given. In fact feudal rent does provide the exploiter with forms of control of the means of production and of the reproduction of the conditions of production of the labourer.[5] Similarly, the nature of the *economy* is not a given – it must be conceptualised for each mode of production. All forms of the economy are not like the capitalist economy, nor are they reducible to technique. The difficulties which arise from Marx's strictly illustrative separation of capitalism and pre-capitalist forms are compounded if these limited remarks are taken as the point of departure for a theory of pre-capitalist modes of production. Once these difficulties are recognised and problematised it becomes necessary to attempt the theoretical construction of *concept* of the economy for various modes of production. Barry Hindess and I have attempted to begin this task in our book *Pre-Capitalist Modes of Production*. Anderson chooses another path, to abandon these Marxist concepts and to adopt a position in which 'modes of production' are generated by the empiricist investigation of historical state constitutions.

Anderson's general conception of pre-capitalist modes of production excludes the articulated combination of forces and relations of production from consideration; however, in his specific discussion of the 'general crisis' of European feudalism he does make a certain use of the forces and relations of production couple. Anderson argues:

> For one of the most important conclusions yielded by an examination of the great crash of European feudalism is that – contrary to widely received beliefs among Marxists – the characteristic 'figure' of a crisis in a mode of production is not one in which vigorous (economic) forces of production burst triumphantly through retrograde (social) relations of production, and promptly establish a higher productivity and society on their ruins. On the contrary, the forces of production typically tend to *stall* and *recede* within the existent relations of production; these then must themselves first be radically changed and resolved *before* new forces of production can be created and combined for a globally new mode of production. In other words, the relations of production generally change *prior* to the forces of production in an epoch of transition and not vice versa. (*Passages*, pp. 203–4)

This passage *inverts* the evolutionist conception of the forces of production bursting through the 'fetter' of the existing production relations. The theoretical effect of the evolutionist conception – authorised by the '1859 Preface' – is to disarticulate the forces/relations combination and install a teleology of technical-cultural progress as the basis of history. Evolutionism supposes the constant tendency of the forces of production to develop in a progressive direction, all relations based on private property must ultimately become 'fetters' on this progress. As a consequence the development of the forces of production determines the course of history; the development of the forces of production is a pan-historical tendency exercised through the structure of modes of production but independently of them. This progress can be grounded in technicism or humanism (the creativity of human nature). The development of the forces is derived from pan-historical attributes and is not a specific effect of the structure of social relations. This evolutionism displaces the role of the political level in transition and the determining role of the class *struggle* – the class struggle is a subordinate effect of a master cause, its outcome is settled in advance. Anderson, always acute to recognise the political consequences of theoretical positions, is opposed to this evolutionism for this very reason.

Anderson's recognition leads him to an *inversion* of this evolutionism and not to its *destruction*. The 'stalling' and 're-cession' of the forces of production are set up to provide the interval or crisis in which politics plays the decisive role. In 'normal' times we presume the forces evolve as before. It is characteristic that Anderson introduces this notion as a conclusion to his analysis of the 'general crisis' of the European feudal economy in the fourteenth century. The general theoretical consequences are not thought out but are allowed to follow from an 'empirical' case. Anderson has no reason to suppose that 'stalling' is characteristic of 'crises' other than this supposed continental recession of the European feudal economies. Any intelligent empiricist will tell you that the events of one case can never tell you anything certain about another. Anderson's position is an empiricist generalisation, and such generalisations are hypothetical.

What is the nature of this 'stalling'? It is a crisis of overpopulation in which feudal agriculture reaches the limits of the cultivable area. Why this should be a crisis of the feudal mode of production *per se*, an index of the retardation of the forces of production necessary to it, escapes me. Why the feudal mode is incapable of further developing the productivity of agriculture even if all cultivable land is occupied is unclear. In the feudal mode tenants do have a direct relation to the instruments of production and methods of working (they are not separated from them in the same way as in the capitalist mode) and tenants, under certain conditions, can derive a definite economic advantage from increasing the productivity of their labour on the land which they rent. Under certain conditions landlords have an interest in increasing the productivity of labour on demesne lands (where these exist). The social conditions favourable to more efficient or intensive working (at least to a certain level) exist in feudal production. Japanese feudal agriculture developed a complex and intensive culture of rice; this demonstrates that the technical form and level of productivity of feudal agriculture are by no means circumscribed in narrow limits. Anderson tries to turn the economic difficulties of the fourteenth century (such as they are) into a necessary 'crisis' of the feudal mode of production.

Even accepting that feudal agriculture reaches the limits of the cultivable area *and* of agricultural productivity in certain regions, such as Britain, then the development of the feudal mode in other regions would be unaffected. Anderson does not claim a general European exhaustion of land reserves, nor is there any hope of claiming an integrated 'European' economy in this period. Local 'crises' could not produce a general crisis. Indeed, land-hungry peasants from the critical areas would provide a labour force for development at the margins where land reserves were abundant.

Anderson defends this notion of a continental 'crisis' by linking the East to the dynamic of the West. Anderson argues that Eastern feudalism was dependent on the West and 'that there was the sudden faltering of the whole economic and demographic impulse transmitted by it' (*Passages*, p. 247). Supposing that this dependence were the case, and that 'there was a synchronic depression in both parts of Europe' (*ibid.*), why is it that the West was incapable of exporting its surplus population as feudal colonists or Eastern landlords incapable of obtaining or attracting labourers from areas of land hunger? Anderson is forced to argue that this is because of a 'demographic collapse' (*Passages*, p. 246) following from the 'stalling' of the forces of production. But, however one stretches the case, 'demographic collapse' cannot be attributed to this cause (even if the downturns in population growth and economic activity *prior* to the plagues are correct). The Black Death is the prime cause of 'demographic collapse'. Plague bacilli are not to my knowledge part of any specification of the forces of production of the feudal mode of production. Anderson turns a conjuncture of expansion in certain regions toward the limits of cultivation and a series of epidemics on a continental scale into a crisis stemming from the necessary 'stalling' of the feudal forces of production. Theoretical positions emerge as generalisations from the most dubious historical analyses.

(iv) The legacy of Eastern 'backwardness' and the October Revolution

Lineages is organised around the attempt to divide Absolutism into distinct Eastern and Western types, characterised by 'divergent trajectories' (*Lineages*, p. 9). Of the three Eastern absolutisms – the Austrian, the Prussian and the Russian – only Russia conforms to Anderson's classic 'Eastern' type. Austria 'never succeeded in creating a coherent and integrated state structure comparable to that of its Prussian and Russian rivals' (*Lineages*, p. 299), it is a 'hybrid' of Eastern and Western forms. Prussian absolutism is transformed into a capitalist state, largely through contact with the more developed Western social relations of the Rhineland. Only Russia persists as the classic 'Eastern' absolutism.

The Russian state in the early twentieth century was still a feudal Absolutist state. Anderson concludes that:

> If all this is so, it is necessary to have the courage to draw the consequences. *The Russian Revolution was not made against a capitalist state at all.* The Tsarism which fell in 1917 was a feudal apparatus: the Provisional Government never had time to replace it with a new or stable bourgeois apparatus. The Bolsheviks made a *socialist revolution* but from beginning to end they never confronted the *central enemy* of the workers' movement in the West. (*Lineages*, p. 359)

Here is the main point of Anderson's prolonged attempt to demonstrate a distinct Eastern variant of Absolutism and to argue that the autonomous development of capitalism is confined to the West. Why was the February revolution not a *bourgeois* revolution? Because the *institutional* forms of the state apparatus were not thoroughly transformed. Anderson derives the class character of the state from the form of its apparatuses. Marxism has classically designated the form of the state by the class which is dominantly represented in it. State apparatuses are agencies of state power, they have a definite effectivity, but the *class* character of a state is defined by the mode in which it exercises state power, by the politics which those apparatuses serve. In what sense is the feudal landlord class the *dominant* class politically represented by the Provisional Government? The class character of the Russian state between the February and October Revolutions can only be analysed at the political level, and this analysis must be in terms of its policies and its practice. Because the Provisional Government did not and could not convert itself into a stable bourgeois republic does not mean that the October Revolution was not made against a state representing the bourgeoisie and its political allies.

This analysis recalls another. The limitations of Russian social-ism for Anderson centre on its failure to confront the bourgeoisie; the non-development of bourgeois democracy bequeaths to the East a legacy of authoritarianism and statism derived from its direct ancestor, the feudal state. The backwardness of the British Left, its lack of theory and its 'corporatism' stem from the failure of the British bourgeoisie to confront the feudal order and in doing so to produce its own conscious and oppositional totalisation, a distinctly *bourgeois* culture or world outlook. The British working class is limited by the absence of the legacy of a class-conscious revolution-ary bourgeoisie, by the resulting amorphousness and detotalising character of the prevailing ideologies. In 'The Origins of the Present Crisis', the text to which we are referring, the French Revolution is the norm of political development – the classic form of a class-conscious bourgeoisie – against which English conditions and their outcomes are secretly measured. In *Lineages* it is Western develop-ment as a whole which is the norm – only in the West is there autonomous capitalist development and a bourgeois-democratic state. The structure of argument is the same. A certain political condition – Russian statism in the one case, British 'backwardness' in the other – is a function of a failure of the working-class movement to confront a class-conscious bourgeoisie under bour-geois-democratic conditions; in the one case it is democracy which is absent, in the other bourgeois class-consciousness.

The real key to Anderson's political concerns, the concerns which illuminate the object of *Passages-Lineages*, is to be found in his essay 'Problems of Socialist Strategy'. Here 'Leninist' strategy and politics, as conceived by Anderson, are reduced to a function of the political and economic backwardness of Russia:

[T]he real historical ground of Soviet Communism was neither despotism, nor collectivism, it was *scarcity*. ('Problems', p. 226)

Russian statism is necessary because '"Civil Society" is so proto-plasmic, disarticulated, amorphous', the state substitutes for and provides 'form' to this 'inchoate magma' ('Problems', p. 228). The West is quite different in its level of political and social develop-ment:

> For the societies of Western Europe constitute a wholly different universe from those of Eastern Europe, let alone Asia. Their highly advanced economies and their complex, dense, tessellated histories have created a social and cultural world entirely of its own. The great political achievement of this world has been democracy. ('Problems', p. 230)

Hence the conclusion:

> Leninist strategy in the West is fundamentally *regressive*: it threatens to destroy a vital historical creation [democracy, PQH], when the task is to surpass it. . . . Leninism . . . is refused by the whole cultural texture of the advanced capitalist societies of the West. (*ibid.*)

Here is the reason for Anderson's concern with the uniqueness of the West, with the singularity of its capitalism and the parliamen-tary democracy sustained by it. Paradoxically, *Passages-Lineages* is about the state in a most fundamental sense. The object of *Passages-Lineages*, the uniqueness of the West as the origin of capitalism, is important because Western capitalism gives rise to democracy. In 'Problems' Russia's statist socialism is ascribed not to despotism but scarcity; in the later text despotism in the form of the legacy of Absolutism is the source of Soviet socialism.

Anderson's project resembles the long line of sociological and historical interpretative attempts to make democracy a unique attribute of the West. In conceiving democracy as the creation of a unique 'trajectory' and the social totality which results from it Anderson essentialises its conditions of existence. Democracy becomes an essential attribute of a type of social structure. Western Europe in this century has also produced Fascism and Nazism, Bonapartist and plebiscitarian regimes – democracy is the fragile product of political struggle. The politics of the European states are not given in some epochal development from a unique origin, rather they are the product of a complex contemporary class struggle whose conditions are changing as new national and

international conjunctures develop. Leninism I take to be precisely
such a rejection of the essentialisation of politics and an insistence
on the analysis of the current conjuncture. Far from being a
dogmatic combination of insurrectionism and statism Lenin's
practice is based upon the principled adjustment of political forms
of struggle to the theoretically analysed conditions of struggle.[6]
Leninist strategy, in this sense, far from being 'fundamentally
regressive' is vital in Britain and the West today. Only by breaking
with the essentialism and evolutionism of the British Left will it be
possible to begin to create a socialist political movement with any
prospect of engaging the current situation with an appropriate
politics. Anderson raises quite correctly in 'Problems' the strong
political commitment of the working class to democratic forms in
contemporary Britain. He was quite right to argue that the Left
must come to terms with the conditions of political struggle under
stable bourgeois-democratic forms, without falling into reformism
pure and simple. A Leninist analysis, far from insisting on
conspiracy and insurrectionism, would attempt to do this. Anderson's mode of analysis and explanation renders this task of political
analysis and the formation of appropriate forms of struggle
impossible.

   Anderson's method and his original conception of the strategy of
the *New Left Review* form a unity. There is no real change in
method between 'The Origins' and *Passages-Lineages*. In both texts
certain objects of analysis are ascribed to a 'trajectory', to
development from an origin. 'Trajectory' is inscribed within a
narrative and the singularity of this narrative is defended and
demonstrated by speculative empiricism. Anderson has been
committed to explanation through genealogy since his first major
text. The result of this explanation through historisation is to
necessitate certain political conditions as the product of a unique
trajectory. This explanation 'places' these conditions but it does not
explain the modality of their current existence. What it is that is
explained or necessitated is not subjected to critical analysis by the
method. Thus the point of departure of 'The Origins' is a very
ambiguous notion of the failure of the British Left and the notion of
'crisis' or malaise reflected in bourgeois popular works. The
method is the historical rationalisation rather than the political
analysis of the current situation. The political conditions of the
present are necessitated as the product of their past but this

necessitation yields no more knowledge about the present than the ideological notions which formed its point of departure. The current situation is not analysed – untheorised or reflected notions about it are historicised.

Hence the abstraction and culturalism of *NLR*'s strategy. Analysis provides no strategic guidance for action in the current situation. That situation is ascribed its essential characteristics by a history. Given Anderson's method and his commitment to socialism the paralysing effects of the past must be effective at the *cultural* level. Culture must determine politics. If it did not then political practice would be necessarily impossible. The weakness of the left would be a necessary feature of the social structure of British Capitalism bequeathed to us by the history of its formation. Culture, however formed by the past, is capable of change – *ideas* can be imported whereas social structures cannot. The political backwardness of the British Left is ascribed to the cultural effects of a history, the effects of the absence of a class-conscious bourgeoisie. *NLR* prescribes a project of cultural enlightenment as the solution to that legacy. This remedying of the defects of English culture, the importation of Marxism, is the sole political practice logically connected with the historical analysis and made possible by it. The cultural products of other histories make good the effects of Britain's unique development. The importance of foreign culture in *NLR*'s project is no accident; it is a necessary result of this analysis and strategy.

Given the predominantly cultural content of the analysis, and its justificatory rather than explanatory relation to the current situation, it is always abstract. Strategy can never change without reconstructing the history, installing a new abstraction. Enlightenment is an endless task, without conditions of fulfilment – the strategy is a timeless one. In a curious way this mirrors the structure of politics generated by another essentialism – that of certain forms of Trotskyism. In this position the current conjuncture is ever always 'objectively' revolutionary, only the 'subjective' conditions are absent due to the failure of the working class to recognise the traitorous nature of their existing political representatives. In the one case 'consciousness raising' unlocks an essentially revolutionary situation by enlightening an essentially revolutionary class. In the other the anti-revolutionary cultural effects of a history are to be combatted by the theoretical enlightenment of the intelligentsia.

This strategy is operative whatever the specific economic and political conditions.

But the current situation refuses to disappear; political situations and struggles are not abolished in the concrete as they are in the abstraction of the strategy. Anderson's position is condemned to culturalism and opportunism. All other political practice than 'enlightenment' must have other sources than his analysis and method. Culturalism and opportunism form a couple – hence *NLR*'s ad hoc adjustment to Labourism in 1964, to the student movement in the late 1960s and, more recently, to the upsurge of Trotskyism.

In spite of this, *NLR* and Anderson did play a progressive political and theoretical role until recently. Whatever the limitations of the analysis from which it sprang, *NLR*'s struggle to raise the theoretical level of the British Left was necessary. No other journal combined a serious relation to theory with an anti-dogmatic and non-partisan programme of presenting the various forms of European Marxism; in particular it was free both of anti-Communism and of the necessity to defend Orthodox Marxism and the legacy of Stalin. *NLR*'s failure is not to be located at the level of its flirtation with Trotskyism nor of its increasing hostility to Althusser and those influenced by him. Its strategy, capable of disseminating Marxism, is not able to use it. It could not exploit its own progressive effects without abandoning its strategy and the method on which it is based, without dissolving itself. This latest text of the *NLR*'s key thinker shows that the relation to Marxism has not changed.

Notes

1 For a striking testimony to Anderson's commitment to the historian's practice see his apologia for relying on secondary works rather than original sources in the Foreword to *Passages*, p. 3.
2 *New Society*, January 30, 1975. For MacRae, Anderson's commitment to the 'comparative method' is what is *valuable* in Anderson's text and the fact that this displaces Marxism a virtue.
3 We will assume here that only modes of production with exploitative relations of production and class domination are combined, for simplicity's sake. Clearly, primitive communist forms can be subordinated in colonial and tributary relationships –

this does not change the general point and merely complicates the exposition.

4 N. Poulantzas, 'Marxist Political Theory in Great Britain', 'Components'. For a demonstration that Anderson's problematic remained unchanged by these apparently 'structuralist' concepts see M. Gane, 'Althusser in English'.

5 These theses are developed and argued in the chapter on the feudal mode in *Pre-Capitalist Modes of Production*.

6 For an able analysis of the concept of the 'current situation' in Lenin see M. Gane, 'Lenin and the Concept of Conjuncture'.

Chapter 6

Interview with *Local Consumption**

Introduction

Texts which bear the singular or collective signatures of Hussain, Hindess, Cutler or Hirst have become noticeable within the context of Marxist theory and politics for a particular mode of theoretical criticism and analysis. To some extent the central questions addressed in these texts have arisen from an intensive investigation and critique of Althusser's theoretical projects. Works like Hindess and Hirst's *Pre-Capitalist Modes of Production* (hereafter *PCMP*) and *Mode of Production and Social Formation* (hereafter *MPSF*) attempted to critically develop Althusserian modes of political analysis, whilst *Marx's Capital and Capitalism Today* (hereafter *MCCT*) – the two-volume collaborative work of all four authors mentioned above – is written very much in the spirit of Althusser and Balibar's *Reading Capital*. Like *Reading Capital*, *MCCT* supplemented its criticism of Marxist theory with far-reaching theoretical and political strategies.

It is inappropriate to associate these texts and authors with 'Althusserianism' as a general philosophy. Their initial concern was to 'use' Althusser's work as a means of political analysis. Another aspect which distinguishes them from the main tendencies of Althusserian influence in relation to areas like ideology is the extent to which 'the critique of epistemology' figured in their theoretical strategy. Briefly the critique of epistemology involved rejecting the conception of knowledge as the apprehension of something which exists independently of discourse. The point was not to choose

*First published in 'Sex, Politics and Representation', edited by Peter Botsman and Ross Harley, *Local Consumption*, Series 5.

between different epistemologies (e.g. idealism or materialism) but to reject epistemological postulates in their diversity. Althusser's conception of a Marxist science was accordingly rejected.

This had a radical effect on Hindess, Hirst, Cutler and Hussain's delimitation of Marxist theory and politics. The rejection of Althusser's 'Marxist science' was not precipitated by speculation about 'metaphysical voids' or a 'crisis in belief'. Nor did it involve embracing alternative 'spontaneist' or 'libertarian' political or theoretical premises. For Althusser's criticisms of 'opportunism' and 'humanism' were well heeded even if his final design was rejected. In this sense Althusser's 'failure' signified the importance of constructing a new set of working parameters for Marxism.

The important result of the critique of epistemology was the position that once epistemological guarantees were rejected the relevance and status of theory should be primarily decided by theoretical debate. Aspects of Marxist theory which had been previously privileged could no longer be automatically endorsed. For example, the concept of mode of production which had been the linchpin of Althusser's analytic model was exposed to criticism and finally rejected. It was argued that the conception of social order as an ordered hierarchy of instances and elements which formed a cohesive unity (e.g. base-superstructure) required the epistemological presupposition of an extra- or pre-discursive totality. The question that was raised here was: 'why should the conditions of social existence give rise to some kind of necessarily ordered totality or unity?'

In *MCCT* these criticisms are developed in the form of a set of radical working proposals for the theorisation of class, the enterprise, economic calculation and the political prospects of socialism. Whilst a good deal of controversy has been associated with these proposals, the theoretical premises and positions developed in *MCCT* have become increasingly important.

Local Consumption interviewed Paul Hirst in the latter part of 1982. The interview traces through some important influences on Hindess and Hirst's earlier works. It also looks at the problems and developments of Marxist theory which are signalled in *PCMP*, *MPSF* and *MCCT*.

L.C. After your many problematisations of Marxist theoretical concepts and frameworks do you still consider yourself a Marxist?

P.H. Many people approach the question of Marxism in terms of whether there is some sort of fundamental talisman by which one can differentiate between Marxists and non-Marxists. Such as, does one subscribe to 'the determination of the economy in the last instance'? The difficulty here is that the people who think that is a sufficient test are confronted with the problem that it is only sufficient for them in our context. So that, for example, many Marxists at the turn of the century would regard a formulation like the 'determination by the economy in the last instance', if rigorously expressed as in Althusser, as inherently revisionist and therefore not Marxist.

Now the point is that it is absolutely useless to pursue Marxism as if there were some simple test by which one could decide whether or not someone is a Marxist. If one looks at contemporary Marxism, it has differentiated to an amazing degree. So that one finds, for example, Edward Thompson arguing for a highly idealist and culturalist version of Marxism which is acceptable because it leaves certain slogans and political investments undisturbed. Whereas other people like ourselves have been concerned to challenge certain aspects of Marxist theory and have not left those political investments undisturbed.

The only way one can sensibly construe the word 'Marxist' is to ask oneself whether the positions that one develops in theory are intelligible except by reference to a long Marxist tradition and criticism and debate within it, and whether one's relation to politics is one such that theory, socialist theory, attempts to assess the political possibilities and to therefore constrain and limit the forms of politics that one is committed to. On both of those counts I would consider myself a Marxist.

Socialist theory must always be a means of assessing states of affairs, of providing a political analysis of the current situation. In that respect, the unity of theory and practice that Marxism has argued for is correct. It cannot be set up, however, in terms of claiming that Marxism is a body of relatively stable scientific truths which can be applied to politics to provide a correct line. There is no 'correct' line.

We are faced with a problem of constructing a socialism which does involve principles, which does argue for priorities on the basis of values, but does not regard itself as a moral crusade which sets out to realise, unambiguously, certain values. Rather principles, priorities and values are used to assess complex political situations in order to discover the domains of possible advance. I regard this as a continuation of a project of scientific socialism, the rectification of the mistakes or limitations in original conceptions of scientific socialism. And so I would call myself a Marxist and somebody whose Marxist theory is crucial to their socialism.

L.C. What is there left in the socialist tradition that is worth pursuing? Is there any point in the strategy of a socialised economy that is regulated by central agencies and planning bodies?

P.H. Those questions seem to me as relevant as they ever were. The need for the socialisation of the economy has become more and more important as national economies have increasingly become directed by central state policy. The question is not whether there are forms of public ownership, planning and state direction − but the *character* of those forms. Now it's at that point that socialist values and priorities are differentiated from those of capitalist rationalisers. Socialist priorities are surely concerned with the following things. One is that the direction of production is based on providing the maximum amount of useful products and services that meet the urgent needs of the people. Another is that in so far as this is possible (and it always involves complex institutional forms and not a simple repetition of the slogan of popular democracy) popular control is essential in expressing what those needs of the people are and in directing the ways that they be met.

It seems to me perfectly clear that socialist principles and priorities are still of value in assessing the ways in which we use instruments like planning, collective ownership, the state direction of the economy in order to achieve various social and economic objectives. So in that sense I see no problem about arguing that the political project of socialism is as relevant as it ever was, that there is no problem of retaining a theoretically informed socialism which in effect is a Marxism, even though the traditional conceptions of a transition from capitalism to socialism are increasingly problematic.

L.C. Lenin still seems to figure, even now in your works, as an exemplary theoretical strategist who worked with success on political issues and problems. Why was Lenin such a prominent reference in your early works? What do you make of *Theoretical*

Practice's Leninist motto 'without revolutionary theory there can be no revolutionary movement' now?

P.H. Traditional Leninism is no longer applicable in a society governed by relatively stable forms of parliamentary democracy. The conditions of such parliamentary struggles have to be assessed anew without merely repeating Lenin's positions as formulas. However, despite this there are two reasons why Lenin remains an influence for those people who started *Theoretical Practice*. The first is that what Lenin tried to do was to think out the *conditions* of different political practices. It was Lenin's practice not to take existing struggles or existing institutions or forms of organisation for granted. In this respect we too must look for new possibilities of political development in relation to new conditions of struggle. This is the spirit of Leninism and it must be retained even in a strategy which is not traditionally 'Leninist' in the sense that it is not primarily concerned with promoting a revolutionary destruction of the existing forms of state. The second point is that Lenin's political theory was neither static nor dogmatic. The later Lenin, the Lenin of the very last writings, was actually trying to figure out the conditions under which a socialist political programme was possible in a society which could not be rapidly socialised and in which the socialist forces faced the enormous mass of the Russian peasantry who could only proceed at a slow pace of genuine change. Lenin's later works were concerned with assessing what that pace and direction of change could realistically be in relation to a powerful constellation of essentially conservative social forces. Lenin recognised that those forces were in no sense inherently socialist or destined towards socialism, they had to be transformed by an appropriately cautious political practice.

In a similar way one can look, in a Leninist sense, at conditions which are different from those of Russia but which pose analogous problems, that is, advanced Western industrial countries. In such societies a majority of the social forces involved are in no sense committed to, or inherently open to socialisation. At which point it is absolutely essential to investigate what are the prospects of political advance and political co-operation with those social forces, bearing in mind that the destruction of parliamentary democracy and its replacement by a new form of state is politically impossible.

It is worth saying that the traditional opposition between a so-called revolutionary road and the parliamentary road is fundamentally ambiguous. Because there is *no* parliamentary road. The conditions of parliamentary struggle are as difficult as those of revolutionary struggle and it is perfectly clear that if one takes the specificity of those political conditions seriously one cannot say that struggle within parliamentary forms will necessarily lead to socialism. So the idea of a definite parliamentary 'road' is an illusory one and anybody who subscribes to the idea of such a 'road' is engaging in unguarded optimism. The question is what are the available forms of political struggle which socialists can engage in which actually carry forward certain of the political principles and the political programmes of socialism even if they do not necessarily lead to the development of a socialist society in which the means of production, distribution and exchange are controlled by the associated producers and in which the state is eliminated.

At this point a fundamentalist interlocutor might object and say: 'This is not a revolutionary position'. The objection would be both correct and idle. The fundamental question is: what are the actual possibilities of a revolutionary transformation? If they are small or non-existent then one must consider other political options. In other words the opposition revolutionary road/parliamentary road radically simplifies our political dilemma. In advanced industrial countries at the present time one is faced with a simple choice: either one tries to develop the most progressive potentialities within existing forms of politics or one condemns oneself to muttering the slogans of a revolutionary sect.

Faced with that choice one has to consider the value of the progress the socialist movement can realistically make. This is a problem which cannot be considered simply in terms of the question: 'what is our ideal society?' Socialism is organised both around a set of principles and a political programme with certain objectives. But the political situations socialists encounter are not of their own making and are not transformable simply because socialists happen to have certain values, wishes or objectives. In which case one is committed to assessing the possibilities of using the principles, the priorities, the programmes of socialism to make limited progress which may provide the basis for further advance. I would argue that the assessment of political conditions in a rigorous way, the adaptation of theory to those conditions, the theorisation of the possibility of struggles and the refusal to conduct politics simply at the level of slogans and illusory hopes are actually Leninist positions. It was Lenin after all who attacked the use of the revolutionary phrase and ultra-left slogan mongering, albeit in a very different political situation. It seems to me that in the current situations in the advanced industrial countries to insist on a 'revolutionary road', to counterpose oneself to an allegedly reformist 'parliamentary road', is to engage in sloganising and phrase mongering.

L.C. Althusser was effectively dropped by many French intellectuals in the 1960s, decisively after May '68, yet in both your own and Barry Hindess's works and in *MCCT* his work continued to be a major object of focus. What is/was the status of Althusser's work for you? What were the priorities behind the lingering attraction?

P.H. To say that Althusser was effectively dropped by many French intellectuals decisively after May '68 is in some ways true but also highly problematic. Some of the more gifted of Althusser's followers, like Rancière, did indeed do this, but they moved over to a libertarian, and in my view ultra-left politics. But one of the problems with assessing Althusser's influence in French politics is that Althusserian theory was politically circumscribed by the conditions that the French CP imposed. So you can't derive directly from Althusser's theoretical positions his personal politics. Althusser's own politics in the CP right up until his open criticism of the leadership and his co-operation with dissidents like Ellenstein avoided direct confrontation with the leadership. The impact of Althusser's theory was always politically limited in France by Althusser's acceptance of the conditions of struggle in the CP.

The second point about Althusser's theory and its impact on intellectuals in France is that those intellectuals have been particularly subject to the dictates of fashion. So that, for example, Marxism at the moment in France is not a popular political theory. It seems to me that in order to assess Althusser's significance one must not take his reception by French intellectuals as a key criterion. Here it is interesting to note that Althusser's theoretical success is primarily not in France but in the Anglo-Saxon countries where Althusser did decisively influence Marxist theory and challenged the forms of theoretical and political humanism which had hitherto prevailed. This was, in general, a very healthy influence.

So in a sense, theoretical humanism, although it was what Althusser was battling against in France, was a more crucial object in the Anglo-Saxon countries and the battle has continued to the present day. What Althusser did was to force people to look again at the nature of Marxist intellectual work, to see it not as a philosophy of social criticism based on certain general metaphysical assumptions about man and history, but rather as a political theory and to consider the ultimate role of theory as providing a means of assessment of political situations. In that sense Althusser did try to link the radical reform of Marxist theory with a Leninist political position. Now however inadequate the substantive elements of Lenin's work may be today that attempt I referred to earlier, to rigorously work out the conditions of politics and to assess them theoretically, is compatible with Althusser's idea of Marxism as a political theory which assesses the current situation.

The problem is that Althusser's influence has become too diffuse. In the Anglo-Saxon countries Althusser's Marxism has been highly influential in the social sciences and in the field of culture but as a general philosophical system and alternative metaphysics. As a methodology but not as a means of analysis of political situations. The amount of Althusserian political theory in that sense is very small.

Theoretical Practice was the main reception in the Anglo-Saxon countries of that conception in Althusser of Marxism as fundamentally a theory of politics and as providing theoretical tools for the assessment of political situations. The problem is, then, that Althusser has been widely influential but that influence has been a general cultural influence. Now it should be said here that *Theoretical Practice* and the people who developed its work, like Barry Hindess and myself, have been forced, in order to try and retain what is positive in Althusser's political theory, to criticise the elements of a general metaphysics in Althusser – to challenge Althusser's theory of the social totality, his conception of epistemology and so on. So that the paradox is that those people who tried to develop the Leninist aspect of Althusser have been the most far-reaching critics of Althusser's philosophy. And in that sense they have broken most radically with many of Althusser's substantive theoretical positions while attempting to work in the spirit in which he started.

L.C. What were the context and priorities behind the work you and your colleagues have done in relation to Marxist theory in *PCMP*, *MPSF* and *MCCT*?

P.H. Our work is primarily an attempt to come to terms with certain theoretical positions that became crucial in Britain in the late 1960s and early 1970s. In particular two could be said to be crucial. One is the Leninist conception of Marxism, and the other is Althusser's attempt to reconstruct Marxist theory. Now in a sense the work of my colleagues and myself has moved away dramatically from our initial concerns.

We started off concerned to produce a Marxist-Leninist theory of politics and to use Althusser's theory as the means to do this. In the course of our work we've been led to substantially criticise, revise and change both of those conceptions and to perceive that Leninism was not a theoretical tradition which in fact could be reconstructed to deal with the political conditions in advanced industrial countries where forms of parliamentary democracy prevailed. And on the other hand, that Althusser's attempt to restructure Marxism and to provide it with a coherent theoretical base was in effect a dramatic failure. It is my view that that was not something to be condemned on Althusser's part. Althusser's failure was extremely important. In failing, Althusser did something which is theoretically more progressive and more significant than virtually any other Marxist thinker. That is, he pushed forms of Marxist theorisation to the limits where their problematic nature became evident.

Now having accepted that Althusser's own work had effectively placed on one side various other positions in Marxism, we started off from the assumption that many aspects of the Althusserian critique of certain forms of Marxism were correct, even if some of the bases from which they were made were fundamentally inaccurate. But the work led in a direction which we never anticipated when it started.

When one looks, for example, at *MCCT*, it was originally intended as a rectification of *Capital* plus certain of the works of Lenin and Hilferding. But in the course of doing so the scale of the problems that emerged seemed to us more considerable than could ever be handled in terms of a rectification. Let me give you a few examples. In the beginning we attempted to develop the work on the theory of value we had begun in *Theoretical Practice* in a way that would put the question of value on one side. That is, we did not regard tackling the philosophical problems about the theory of value as the crucial problem. However, we rapidly perceived that unless one tackled these problems there would always be grounds for saying 'these people have not understood value'. One finds a traditional critique which always reduces criticisms to pre-Marxist positions, like the critique of Sraffa's work which contends that it is neo-Ricardianism. We wanted to disrupt the idea that there was present in *Capital* an adequate theory of value from which other positions were a deviation. Similarly, to begin with, we attempted to reformulate and reconstruct the various tendencies in *Capital* such that we could produce a position on tendency which would be more sophisticated than Balibar's and yet which would reformulate and save the various tendencies identified at different points in the three volumes of *Capital*. Now of course that work broke down as well. So the project as it started off was rather more conservative than the results that were eventually produced. The point of the style of work we adopted was to take up ruthlessly certain forms of theoretical argument and pursue their implications willy-nilly, without regard either to the results in terms of a body of established texts or to certain political expectations that one had. And of course the results were in many cases as distressing for us as they have been for other people who read our books.

One of the implications of *MCCT* is that there is no general meta-structure of Marxist theory which can be restored in such a way that we also get a consistent orthodoxy which could be satisfactory in relation to traditional political conclusions of Marxism. Now various other people have in effect moved that way too. There is in a sense very little orthodox Marxism. For example, Perry Anderson's *Lineages of the Absolutist State* is highly unorthodox and actually changes Marxism to a point where certain sociologists said: 'This is a very good book, but why is this man continuing to make special claims for Marxism? It is just good comparative sociology.'

MCCT could be regarded primarily as a negative work, but only if one sets up the following opposition: theoretical criticism is negative, substantive investigation is positive. I would argue that theoretical criticism cannot be considered as negative. People who contrast theoretical critical work to substantive analysis are making a mistake. It is fair to argue that a very great deal of Marx's own work for a very long period consisted in elaborate theoretical criticism and that the destruction of certain theoretical forms by their internal exploration or by their external critique should not be considered as simply negative and be contrasted with the production of positive results. That is, a positivist or scientist view of the virtues of theoretical work.

I would further argue that there is a very great deal in *MCCT* which is not simply of the nature of negative theoretical criticism. A considerable part of it attempts to formulate new theoretical concepts and these have received less attention than the criticism of Marx. In particular it is worth noting that the second volume of *MCCT* is little considered by people who attempt to assess, evaluate or criticise the book, that the attempt to provide a new theory of financial capital, of enterprises, of calculation and so on is not taken seriously by people who are hostile to the thrust of the theoretical criticism. It is worth saying that some colleagues have attempted to develop our work in relation to the theory of the enterprise or finance capital (e.g. the work of Grahame Thompson or Jim Tomlinson).

Further there are important aspects of the first volume, such as the attempt to provide a different kind of theory of classes, which are also positive. Subsequent work, for example, on the subject of parliamentary democracy, the nature of the enterprise, the nature of trade unions and the law cannot be considered as merely theoretical criticisms, even if in many cases it does challenge certain theoretical positions within Marxism. *MCCT* is not merely a critical rejection of certain positions, it is the elaboration of a new and distinct theoretical framework. In that sense we would argue that the exploration of Althusser which we began has produced positive theoretical results. Those results can actually be further developed and elaborated, although they cannot lead to a theory or philosophy of history or a general theory of the social totality linked to such a view of history. People who seek such a theory will always find the products of our distinct kind of theoretical writing wanting. I would argue that that is their problem rather than our failing and in that sense they should adapt to changed conditions of theoretical work and to the collapse of the attempt to provide a general 'science of history' or philosophy of history.

L.C. A fundamental and recurring axis of *MCCT*'s critique of *Capital* is the notion that Marxist theory relies on an epistemological fiat which compels us to conceive of a world which is independent, extra-discursive and yet specifiable in discourse. Could you outline the strategy behind the arguments on epistemology?

P.H. Our critique of epistemology was concerned to challenge certain forms of hegemonisation of the assessment of Marxist discourses by the demand that theory correspond to some extra-theoretical domain, such as a concept of being – that the assessment of theory is the adequacy of correspondence with being. We raised the problem of how that correspondence could be assessed other than by perceiving the object of correspondence as something which existed independently of the theories which constructed that object.

Many people would then go on to argue that we consider that all the world consists of discourse and that we are unwilling to consider something called the 'extra-discursive'. Now this is absurd. The point very simply is that the objects of theory are in a sense constructed within theory, that the objects involved are diverse and that there is no general domain called the 'extra-discursive'. This is not to argue that there are not things which are outside of discourse, argument or theoretical formulations but rather that those things do not have the form of a single 'reality' to which all theories can be measured or correspond. That is, the notion of reality sets up a world of existence which has certain coherent attributes. We would wish to argue that there is no way in which we can assess such a 'reality' because what we actually get when we refer to the objects of distinct theories, sciences or practices is a diverse domain of constructed objects. These do not sum to form something called 'reality' to which those theories can be made, independently of their own constructed objects, to correspond. But this in no sense argues that all there is in the world is theory or discourse or something of this kind.

Further it should be clear that the conception of theory involved in the critique of epistemology that we use is not theory as a set of ideas or propositions but theory as a practice. Theory as a practice which includes theoretically constructed and theorised means of experimentation, that is definite objects like, for example, machines, the re-working of experimental materials for analysis and so on. So our critique of epistemology is not interested in attempting to set up a new metaphysics which reduces everything to discourse – in opposition to a metaphysics which sets up a uniform reality as the measure of diverse forms of discourses and demands that their adequacy can be based on their correspondence with it and that the adequacy of that correspondence determines their truth.

In that respect theoretical argument need not be hegemonised by epistemological discourse. The object of the critique of epistemology was to move away from making epistemology the means of assessment of discourse. Epistemology was considered in quite a specific way, as a theoretical domain that tries to state a mechanism of correspondence between a discourse and objects existing outside discourse which can be specified and made the measure of it. This critique of epistemology in no sense commits one to conceiving of the means of assessing truth in general as coherence within discourse or something of this kind. The point is that concepts of truth as correspondence are what need to be rejected. One can still retain notions of the adequacy of forms of knowledge, of criteria of experiment, forms of evidence, of testing and so on. However, those criteria are based upon convention and agreement as to what is adequate and not on some independently existing 'reality'. There is no rejection in this critique of the assessment of the adequacy of knowledge. The point being made is that assessments, which use evidence, testing, criteria of validity will be diverse and that different forms of evidentialisation, different forms of testing and so on will be adequate to the purposes of the different knowledges involved. In that respect the critique of epistemology is a challenge to a certain view of epistemology that is dominant in Marxism and it has a number of similarities with the critique of certain theories of science and certain theories of truth that one finds in non-Marxist philosophers like Hacking or Quine or Rorty for example.

L.C. *PCMP* started off with a firm position on the general concept of mode of production and sought to apply it. Althusser's concept of social totality was in large part still intact at the end of that work. Then in *MPSF* this standpoint was submitted by yourself and

Barry Hindess to criticism, such that the concepts of mode of production and social totality were seen as unworkable theoretical concepts. In *MCCT* those criticisms were taken even further. How do you now see the theorisation of social structure?

P.H. Totalities and social structures are not the same thing. Totalities have certain general forms of privileged causality which act to secure the conditions of existence of the whole, and so certain necessary states of affairs and a certain future follow from the action of those causalities. To criticise this is not to argue for a wholly disarticulated congeries of autonomous fragments as certain of our critics claim. Social relations are structured, in that they have definite inter-connections between institutions, practices and their conditions, but the mode in which such links exist is different from the privileged determinations postulated by theories of totality and can vary between one time and another. Hence the limits of a 'general theory' do not mean that we cannot consider definite patterns of social relations and their consequences; indeed, this latter problem is just what Penny Woolley and I address in our book *Social Relations and Human Attributes*.

L.C. The position that the evaluation of political issues and platforms can no longer be conceived as a matter of essential class interests and that the problematics of politics and representation are open to question is seen, perhaps not surprisingly, by many Marxists as having gone too far. How would you respond to such reservations?

P.H. The criticism of the concept of representation was concerned to attack certain arguments in which the validity of a set of ideas, or of a political party, or a political practice was considered in terms of the question: does it adequately represent the class from which it derives? Class being considered in the Marxist sense of a group of agents holding a certain relation to the means of production.

The point to be made here is that the critique of representation is not intended to argue that there are *no* relations between social forces and groups in politics – which many people have drawn as a conclusion. This is painstakingly opposed in the course of the arguments. The point is that political groups and classes as social forces are not in fact reducible to being mere expressions of economic classes defined as groups of agents having a common structural relation to the means of production. Such economic groups are abstractions produced in economic analysis and different in nature from classes as social forces. We can continue, however, to use terms like 'working class' bearing in mind that we mean by this in British political discourse certain groups of workers, certain communities and so on. We don't mean by this what Marx means for example by the concept of exploited labour or productive labour. It is quite clear that if we try to use those latter categories then they relate to the social topography of British society spelt out in the discourses of contemporary politics very, very badly. In other words we are arguing that there is a systematic discrepancy between the categories of 'class' we use in everyday political discourses and the Marxist theory of classes based on 'relation to the means of production'. The latter are not social forces, but postulated entities at the level of a general structure of the mode of production.

One can see quite clearly in a number of debates which try to make classes, in the Marxist sense, fit with groups in contemporary politics that these parallelisms break down. Good examples are Poulantzas's attempt to re-draw class boundaries or the debate about the 'middle strata' sponsored by the British CP. In these attempts, the lines of demarcation become progressively dispersed and the distinctions break down.

It should be quite clear that there never was any attempt in our critique of representation to argue that economic groups and forms of politics were completely separate. This type of reading insists on accepting the Marxist theory of the social totality as the only possible measure and assuming that non-correspondence means non-relation. If one were to retain a concept of the totality and to claim that its levels are necessarily disarticulated then this would be an absurd position. However, what we were doing was to argue that one must *reject* theories of totality, of necessary correspondence between economic classes and political forces, and move to analysing specific and contingent connections between classes as social forces and political parties and so on. Our analysis is concerned to avoid postulating the necessary correspondence between objective interests of classes and certain political outcomes. Rather, the point is to analyse what actual interests there are, what actual mechanisms whereby they become effective in politics. So it could be said that the attempt to argue that the critique of representation goes too far, is based, on the one hand, on a tissue of misreadings and, on the other hand, on a demand that our theory fit with pre-conceived Marxist conceptions of social totality.

L.C. At the end of *MCCT* the reader is left, so to speak, with the Labour Party in Britain as 'a crucial area for political transform- ation'?

P.H. It is correct to say that at the end of *MCCT* the reader is left with the Labour Party. *MCCT* is a book with various theoretical and political implications but the conclusion of the book was written in order to apply the theoretical criticisms and theoretical developments in relation to Marxism to a quite specific political situation – that of Britain in the late 1970s. Now the conclusions to the book are in no sense authoritative in relation to the theoretical arguments and they should not be seen as being generally valid for any advanced industrial country.

The Labour Party is central because in assessing the available political forces one is faced with deciding which forces are possible agents of transformation of social relations. It should be quite clear that none of the forces to the left of the Labour Party has any prospect of playing a crucial role in that respect. The CPGB for example, has never been able in the past thirty years to get a single member of parliament elected. The other left parties, sects and factions are even less substantial or successful. The real question here is that the political forces which can effect transformations of social relations are in no sense reducible to political ideals. In that sense people on the left, who claim to be materialists and yet support extremely tiny political parties or sects are themselves idealists.

The Labour Party is important for a number of reasons. It is the only party capable of both being a socialist party and of commanding a majority of the electorate. Secondly, it is the only left party that has had the ability to govern. The fact that the Labour Party is a party of government does involve problems but it also means that the Party has had the political skills, the political experience to walk in and start acting in relation to the state machine. That is, to be perceived as being capable of providing efficient decisions by, for example, managers of the larger private and public corporations, by central civil servants and by officials in local government. Those are the pre-conditions for making any significant changes under parliamentary politics.

The lifetime of parliament in Britain is five years. Reforming parties must deliver fairly rapidly in order to secure political support. If they have to change aspects of the state machine they have to do so while co-operating with the personnel and the procedures of that state machine. Further it is clear that under the dominance of parliamentary democratic forms only substantial structural reforms are possible. You cannot completely socialise the economy and the system of production and distribution by using legislative and administrative instruments in the course of a five-year parliament. The crucial question that faces a party like the Labour Party getting into office is how to act politically in the course of one parliament in order to both achieve a significant programme of reform that addresses certain of the important problems of British society and which provides itself with a means of being re-elected.

Now for all these reasons we took the Labour Party to be central. We took a strategy of substantial structural reforms to be crucial and we questioned, in the course of the conclusion to *MCCT*, certain of the views of how to proceed in the area of structural reforms like those advocated by Stuart Holland and Tony Benn. There is no point in going over those criticisms here. But it is worthwhile saying that the position we took when we published the book, that the Labour Party is the crucial focus of left strategy, has become increasingly the case. That is, large sections of the ultra-left have been driven to define themselves in relation to the Labour Party and to attempt to enter it. In that sense the political dominance of the Labour Party is confirmed rather than denied. So I would argue that when one says that at the end of *MCCT* the reader is left with the Labour Party that is true, and that is something which could not have been otherwise.

L.C. In Australia there has been in some quarters a sort of joint influence of your works with Hindess et al. and Foucault. However in other cases investments in either your works or Foucault's and 'French theory' collide. The conflict, to put it crudely, is between the image of intellectuals diligently chipping away at the Labour Party, Marxist theory and economic theory, etc., and a more mobile set of intellectual pursuits outside of those terrains, at theoretical levels 'on the margins'. I wonder what you make of these conflicts?

P.H. In relation to our own work, we have never been 'Foucauldian'. We have been willing to use Foucault's theoretical work in relation to areas like the history of ideas, to treat it positively and to regard it as a genuine and massive achievement. But never in any sense to attempt to be 'Foucauldian'.

The reasons for this are very straightforward. Foucault's working methods are such that no loyalism or orthodoxy can be erected on the basis of them and anybody who tries to become a 'Foucauldian' is condemned to be a sterile repeater of Foucault's themes. Now we have always been primarily concerned with Marxist theory and we have never regarded Foucault as providing an alternative to Marxism or a comprehensive political and social theory. Certain of Foucault's positions have been strongly influential upon us and we are quite willing to use Foucault's arguments, but we do not treat Foucault as somebody who provides an 'alternative way of looking at things'. This relates back to the question of politics; those people who do see Foucault as providing an alternative way of looking at things are often concerned to propose a libertarian politics which rejects existing forms of political investment and political institutions and argues for limited practices of resistance.

Our reaction to this would be as follows. Firstly, Foucault's own politics do not follow from his theoretical positions. His position is not a general social theory and the attempt to make it so in the libertarian usage of Foucault closes off a number of the most interesting aspects of his work. For example, people who centre on the concept of resistance in Foucault are using a residual category and one which is incoherent. It is worth saying that the concept of resistance cannot deal with some of the fundamental political problems. Foucault is quite correct to attack what he calls the juridico-discursive concept of power. He is also correct to attack the attempt to write down political/social/institutional developments to the interests of social classes. However the reading of Foucault which uses the notion of resistance moving from various points at the periphery to challenge established institutions goes overboard in relation to what the critique is able to substantiate. The point is that Foucault is correct to say that the juridico-discursive concept of power is not an adequate account of either power or the modern state. Yet the state remains a crucial focus and politics organised around states remains central because, not only in relation to the 'social field' which Foucault considers, but in relation to questions of the economic order, the state is a major element in the determination of the political and economic prospects for advanced industrial countries. Now it is correct to challenge the parliamentary cretinism which sees a majority in parliament as providing a control of the state machine – both Hindess and I have argued that states are immensely more complex than either liberals, Marxists or indeed people who follow Foucault can see. And in that sense, the control of state policy and the state machine means coming to terms with a heterogeneous set of institutions which often do not have a coherence in policy or practice. This is not to say that the direction of central state policy is not crucial. It is quite clear, for example, in relation to macro-economic policy that modern national economies are crucially effected by the behaviour of states.

At this point it seems to me impossible to move away from the focus of the state, the political party, the institutions of state administration, the political management of the economy, the social welfare system and so on because nothing Foucault has said reduces the importance of those areas. It remains a fact that these areas impose certain political conditions of institutional struggle. One of these is the need to work through mass parties in order to achieve electoral victories in order to provide certain of the conditions of access to political decision-making. The other is to work through the complex administrative machineries of states themselves such that a variety of effective decisions are produced. Those two practices are not the same, but in both cases one is forced to utilise certain political forms, to wit the politics of the mass electorate and, on the other hand, the politics of administrative reform. These issues remain as important as they ever were – allowing for all the points that Foucault has made about the 'microphysics' of power, for the fact that the state cannot be treated as simply an expression of the sovereign will, whether the 'soveriegn' be a king or the people and so on.

Now one final point in relation to this question on the notion of 'French theory'. It seems to me that very few people now believe in the notion of 'French theory' which prevailed a few years ago –

which was structuralism. But the investment of certain progressive Anglo-Saxon intellectuals in issues that emanate from France continues. I think in this respect we should just forget the notions of 'French theory' or 'structuralism' or any other such slogan and see that these people who do continue to operate as conduits of structuralism, etc. are engaged in a rather abstracted practice which is a contestation in the academic field.

It is worth adding, to come back to the point about conventional political issues, that in the UK the sort of theory we are referring to has not been politically influential, if by that we mean that it has impinged directly in the crucial political issues of the day as they are set up by the major political parties, forces, movements, social institutions and so on. However in relation to the Labour Party the intelligentsia does occupy a crucial place and it can fight for certain political programmes and issues. Now of course that cannot be done in terms of French theory. So that if one does try to adapt one's political position to the prevailing conditions, it must also be clear that it definitely imposes limits on the forms of the radical work and the types of intellectuality involved. In that sense it would be fair to say that conventional politics involves a withdrawal from certain kinds of theoretical concerns – what it imposes is a limitation of the kind of discourse by means of which those concerns are brought into politics. In other words, while certain kinds of theory may actually help in formulating political lines they cannot be used as a means of furthering those lines in the political domains where they are consequential.

L.C. In *PCMP* it was maintained that 'history was not a coherent or worthwhile object of study'. You argued that all political theory, however abstract and general, exists to make possible the analysis of the 'current situation'. Do you still stand by those positions?

P.H. The conclusion of *PCMP* is often read as a kind of statement saying we don't need to do history. History is a load of rubbish. Now that response has come mainly from academic historians who saw themselves as under threat of having an Abolition Act put on their work. A lot of left-wing historians define their practice primarily within the academy. That is, they situate themselves in relation to academic historical writing and see themselves as

providing an alternative to it. What we argued was that, for a
Marxist, this is the wrong approach.

If one conceives Marxism as a political theory concerned to
analyse current situations then the use of history or the reference to
history will always be governed by the political problems that one
perceives in relation to those current situations. In certain cases that
may involve the use of historical work, in others it may not. The
critique of the relevance of history is directed primarily round the
idea that Marxism is a philosophy of history or a general history of
all hitherto existing societies. The argument we wanted to put
forward was that, on the contrary, Marxism is not a science of
history, it is a theory of contemporary politics and its use of history
will always be selective by reason of its political concerns.

So when we said the study of history is theoretically and
politically valueless, that was an extreme way of posing the
problem: theoretically and politically valueless in the sense that
history has no general and necessary relation to a certain kind of
Marxist political project. We did not mean to say that it is
politically and theoretically valueless *per se*. But people left out that
point.

Now I would say that in certain circumstances historical
argument is one of the terms in which political debate is conducted.
So that for example, debates about the Soviet Union which have
very general political resonances concern themselves with what
happened in the 1917 Revolution. That is perfectly reasonable and
I would not want to disagree. But the difficulty is that if one situates
oneself primarily in terms of existing practices of an academic
discipline then one radically reduces one's intellectual mobility in
relation to political problems. One accepts many of the definitions
that the discipline sets up. For this reason, I would want to say that
I would still accept the arguments in *PCMP* although perhaps we
would write them more cautiously now.

Furthermore, if one looks, for example, at the debate with
Thompson, one of the things that emerges very clearly is that
Thompson, whether he likes it or not, does have a philosophy of
history. For him history is set up as an object of a very particular
type. He claims that there is a unique practice, the writing of
history, which produces a singularly valuable kind of knowledge. I
would dispute this. I would argue that the products of the practice
of historiography are exceedingly diverse and that they have to be

analysed piecemeal, not merely by their own historiographical merits but also in terms of their political usefulness.

Now as it happens, in some of my work I make use of a great deal of social history, for example, the debates about witchcraft in early modern Europe in *Social Relations and Human Attributes*. That use is conditional. It is not in any sense a general endorsement of historiography nor is it a general rejection. Furthermore, given your interest in Foucault I should compare his approach to historical writing with our own. I would not say that what we are doing and what Foucault has been doing are the same. On the other hand, I think that one of the most useful things Foucault does is to raise problems about historiography.

The Archaeology of Knowledge, for example, is a fundamental attack on the intellectual presuppositions of a certain kind of history of ideas. Now Foucault's attempt to replace history with 'archaeology' has led to similar kinds of response from academic historians to those you find in relation to our work. For example, historians like Carlo Ginsburg or Erik Midelfort argue that Foucault is a bad and over-selective historian. Foucault's point is that he is concerned with the conditions of possibility of the present, that his selections of historical material are strategic ones. They are governed by certain contemporary problems and they work through trying to identify the emergence of certain strategic discourses.

Now the interesting thing here is that historians tend to assume that he is engaging in an illegitimate selectivity, that if we look at a particular period we find that other things were going on. Of course, that is perfectly true, but that is to treat Foucault's work rather like a general history, as providing a complete description of a period, when of course Foucault is doing nothing of the kind. He is trying to analyse certain historical discourses as strategic in relation to certain problems that he is concerned with. The point is not, as an historian like Midelfort does in his critique of Foucault's analysis of madness, to plead continuity against discontinuity, and to insist on a general description of a period. This is, of course, exactly what Foucault is opposed to. It seems to me that in this respect Foucault and Donzelot are engaged in a very different and much more strategic practice than traditional historiography. When one looks at the details of the case, they do not get things as wrong as some historians claim they do. Thus Foucault is not ignorant of medical therapeutics in relation to mental illness in the Renaissance. One must be very careful of historians' criticisms of Foucault precisely because they take their own practice as a privileged point of departure, which Foucault does not. The debate between Foucault and historians will always be a debate from different positions.

Chapter 7

Labour's Crisis – Principles and Priorities for Social Reconstruction[1]

Why is the Labour Party important? This question must be asked by democractic socialists, rather than take it for granted that Labour is the main vehicle for the attainment of a more equal and just, more democractic and efficient society. It must be asked and honestly answered for two reasons. Firstly, the LP is a declining electoral force, commanding the support of less than a third of the British electorate, and it has faced a serious internal crisis, as evidenced by defections to the SDP and factional fighting between Left and Right, which has further weakened its electoral appeal.

Secondly, there are important strands of thinking on the Left that are highly critical of the LP in its present form, either regarding it as an obstacle to the attainment of revolutionary socialist change, or wishing to concentrate on the development of popular, non-parliamentary forms of politics. At its most extreme the first view, represented by Ralph Miliband and David Coates, sees the decline of Labour as a powerful electoral force as a necessary condition of socialist advance. Labour, it is argued, appears to offer the prospect of socialist politics but in fact it is essentially reformist and therefore incapable of bringing about socialist change. Many of the Labour Left hold to a rather different version of this thesis, in which Labour is basically socialist but perpetually led astray by a wayward parliamentary leadership. On this view, Labour can become a vehicle for socialist politics, but only on condition of radical transformations, restricting the freedom of action of its leadership through 'democratic' reforms and strengthening its working-class base through the development of a mass popular politics. For all their differences both versions share two highly problematic assumptions: firstly, that what Labour governments do in office is largely a function of reformist ideology and orientation, thereby discounting the significance of political, economic and institutional constraints on attainable policies that cannot simply be wished or legislated away; secondly, that there is a potential popular majority for wholesale socialisation. This latter depends on an act of faith in the essential socialism of the working class. There is no serious evidence for this position, and what evidence there is points in a different direction. Over the years, opinion polls have consistently shown a clear majority of the British people hostile to extensive nationalisation, and there is no evidence whatever that they would prefer a more genuine socialisation of the means of production. In addition, there is a real fear that extensive nationalisation may lead to a loss of personal freedom and to forms of authoritarian control more characteristic of the USSR. This cannot be dismissed as a mere illusion, the product of media conditioning; it is a deeply felt and genuinely 'popular' response to political experience.

The latter of the two views is well represented by the authors of *Beyond the Fragments* (Rowbotham, Segal and Wainwright) who envisage the growth and collaboration of a number of extra-parliamentary movements as the basis for left advance. Unfortunately, the movements they have in mind barely touch the mass of the British people. Popular and non-parliamentary politics certainly need to be developed, but they should not be seen as displacing parliamentary and electoral politics or relegating them to a subordinate position. There are urgent social and economic problems in Britain today that must be tackled at governmental level, and the Left cannot afford to neglect them.

But to make these points against those who would reject the LP in anything like its present form is not to make a positive case for it. Labour is far from being either the strategic revolutionary party or the co-ordinator of a mass popular politics that many on the Left would like to see. Why then is the LP important? There are three reasons why the survival and electoral prospects of the LP as a whole, rather than just the political advantage of the Left or Right within it, should be matter of concern for socialists. Firstly, a democratic socialist politics has to take seriously the task of working for its objectives within and through the institutional structures of parliamentary democracy. Secondly, Labour is important as the parliamentary arm of the trade unions. Thirdly, it provides a crucial space for socialist arguments to intervene in the mainstream of British political life. Each of these reasons requires further comment.

(i) A democratic socialist politics in Britain has to recognise and accept the genuine popular commitment to parliamentary democracy and its associated civil and political liberties. Socialists have to take seriously the problems of working for their objectives within and through the institutional conditions of parliamentary democracy, the importance of tackling widely recognised social problems and the need to secure and sustain popular support for and compliance in their policies. Socialists neglect these political problems at their peril. The electoral and parliamentary strengths of a party are therefore of fundamental importance, the one as representing a necessary minimum of popular support and the other as a condition of direct *access* to administrative decisions. We stress *access* here, rather than control, for two reasons. Firstly, it is far from clear that any one party will be in a position to form a government after the next election in 1987 or before. If Labour is to enter government at all, it may have to do so as part of a governing coalition.

Secondly, the notorious slogan attributed to Hartley Shawcross after the 1945 landslide – 'We are the masters now' – embodies a dangerous illusion of power. In the British political system no government can be 'the master'. Governments have to work *through* a complex and intractable state machine and the administrative bureaucracies of the economy. Tony Benn and his associates have drawn the wrong conclusions from their experiences of dealing with the civil service and big business, at least in suggesting that a more centralised and ruthless administrative style is necessary, forcing its decisions through regardless of opposition. This is precisely what the Tories have tried to do. The problem, in a political system like ours, is that such pseudo-authoritarian decisions can and will be unmade after the next general election, if not before. Alienating the leading administrators in national and local government and in industry and a substantial proportion of the electorate who are far from being solid Labour voters would not provide a basis for future advance. Labour must govern by consent, and it must reach and implement decisions by means which overcome rather than promote opposition. The LP has shown it could do this to a satisfactory extent in the immediate post-war period and between 1964–70 and 1974–8. It can and must do so again.

The Labour Party has been an effective *party of government*. It was capable, in the period since 1965 and until the débâcle of 1979, of providing efficient and stable decision-making within the prevailing parliamentary and economic system and, therefore, of commanding the respect of the leading administrators in the civil service and local government and of management in the big public and private corporations. Many on the Left will dismiss this with contempt, but they are unwise to do so. It is a crucial condition for being able to do anything in the way of alternative policies and significant reforms. It stands in clear contrast with the experience of the Tory Party in the post-Macmillan era. Civil servants, local government officials and businessmen are widely resentful and critical of capricious and unpredictable Tory decision-making. The ability to make the system 'work' is a condition for electoral success *and* for its meaningful and acceptable reform.

(ii) The Labour Party is the parliamentary arm of the trade unions: it originated as a means of representing trade union interests in Parliament and it has never lost that role even though it has also developed a distinct mass party machine. There is no doubt that there is an anti-union majority in popular opinion and in the other political parties. Even a majority of trade union members agree, according to opinion poll data, that the unions have 'too much power'. The precise significance of such data may be questioned but it would be foolish to ignore the extent and the genuineness of the popular response. It is one thing to recognise such views and another to capitulate to them, and here the Labour Party faces a crucial task of political education. But it also has the tremendous advantage that Labour alone of all the parties capable of entering government is able to deal with the unions in such a way as to secure their compliance. This was a crucial aspect of the election victory of 1974 and Labour's failure to retain that compliance in the winter of 1978–9 played a significant role in the Labour government's defeat.

We argue, against the consensus, that the trade unions, and the shop stewards' movement in particular, are a healthy and democratic element in British society. Reforms are certainly necessary, but not such as would demobilise the union movement or make it less democratic and less capable of defending its members' interests. It is difficult to prove, but necessary to argue that the growing strength of the trade unions in the post-war period has played a major part in raising the living standards of the mass of the working people and that such a development has been healthy. Most of those on the Left who argue thus then go on to assume that the trade unions can continue as they are, and that major institutional reforms are unnecessary. This is a fundamental error, a form of institutional conservatism which would inhibit the development and transformation of the unions in ways which enhance the overall capacities of working people to preserve their jobs and improve working conditions. We will return to this 'conservatism' which is all too typical of left attitudes, accepting a 'radical' economic programme but refusing to recognise the need for radical changes in institutions and attitudes.

It is also difficult to prove and equally necessary to argue that the trade unions bear a heavy share of responsibility for the widely recognised industrial inefficiency which is at the heart of Britain's economic crisis. That a radical economic programme which tackles Britain's economic crisis must be accompanied by significant changes in working practices is something that much of the Left is unwilling to accept. Such changes need not be merely at the service of management prerogatives. The unions are also capable of forming the basis of a genuine industrial democracy which could play a part in revitalising British industry and give new powers and responsibilities to workers. The trade unions are of crucial importance for any attempt at national income planning which, in addition to controlling inflation, sets itself the task of a radical redistribution of income and wealth. Only the Labour Party can provide the basis of confidence and trust on the part of working people and their industrial leaders necessary to carry through such reforms. This is a tremendous long-run political asset.

(iii) Labour is an important forum and vehicle for serious socialists and it provides a crucial space for socialist arguments to intervene and have an impact in the mainstream of British political life. As a party, Labour is doctrinally committed to extending socialisation, to greater equality in the distribution of income and wealth, and to the provision of health, education and welfare on the basis of need. In this respect, Labour remains a *socialist* rather than a *social democratic* party like the German or British SDPs.

However, it is obvious that the Labour Party is not and has never been a strategic revolutionary party. Its whole organisational structure and practices are geared to securing electoral victories. Labour is a *parliamentary party*, still dominated by elected representatives, and a machinery primarily geared to mobilising the mass vote for elections. Its primary extra-parliamentary form remains the trade unions, who in turn are constitutionally and organisationally limited bodies. Further, the Labour Party has always been a complex coalition of factions and interest groups, there has been no period in which the 'Left' or the 'Right' has been wholly subordinated or in which ideological adherence to a 'programme' has been successfully enforced. To many these things will appear glaring blemishes rather than assets. The poor ability to develop and sustain extra-parliamentary struggles *is* a real weakness. But only as a coalition, an electoral machine and a party of competent government, can Labour hope to win elections and hold office.

Labour's programme must be broadly based in order to command electoral success. In this respect, the very complexity of the party is a real asset, for any response to Britain's problems which can command the support of the party as a whole has some chance of convincing the social forces and people of Britain. In this respect, the idea of a 'left' Labour Party, in which other sections of opinion are excluded or restrained, is an illusion. So too is the idea of a 'left' Labour government. The 'Left' has failed to win the party as a whole, despite its growing strength. This should not be seen as an index of the ground that remains to be covered, a residual resistance of the 'Right' which can be subordinated. On the contrary, such resistance has grown with the rise of the 'Left' influence; it reflects not merely conservatism but a recognition of real failures and lacunae in the policies and aspirations of the Left itself. In this respect, the party as a whole remains in touch with the opinions of the British people and the facts of political life. A 'socialist' party which is a complex and divided coalition, not wholly socialist, has strengths and assets in the circumstances of British electoral politics which must not be ignored. The success and dominance of any one element of that coalition would signal the long-run demise of the party; that is as true of the 'Right' as of the 'Left'. For all the elements of genuine 'realism' on the part of the Labour Right and Centre, these sections of the party lack the means, ideas and will to tackle Britain's problems. A combination which combines the strengths of each of the party's factions in a viable programme is the basis for political success. There is some ground for hope that such a prospect exists.

To insist on the fundamental importance of the Labour Party for democratic socialist politics in Britain today is not to say the parliamentary and electoral politics should be the exclusive concern of socialists, merely that they are far too important for socialists to ignore or disparage. But our objectives should not be restricted to what Labour should do in government. They also concern, as our earlier comments on industrial democracy and on the need for major institutional reforms in the unions will have indicated, the politics and practices of the Labour movement. The movement as a whole needs to be capable of adaptive change to new circumstances. The need to extend discussion of 'policies for Labour' beyond 'policies for Labour-in-government' is important not merely because it is by no means certain that Labour *will* form the next government, but because the whole structure of the party and the unions needs to be overhauled in order to effectively link parliamentary and other forms of politics.

Nor is our insistence on the importance of the LP to ignore the political problems it faces. The split which led to the formation of the SDP and the subsequent electoral alliance with the Liberals poses a genuine and serious threat to Labour's electoral prospects. Both the Labour and the Tory parties have steadily lost in their percentage of the vote and are increasingly restricted to regional bases of support and exclusive social constituencies. In all probability, the next election will present a more complex problem than a vote *against* the existing government. Labour no longer occupies the position of an automatic electoral alternative and has to compete with an increasingly effective alternative opposition.

Many hold that the 'leftward' drift of the Labour Party has alienated popular support, that this phenomenon has produced a fear of an 'ideological' party whose policies are dictated by activists rather than the leading parliamentary politicians whom the public knows. However real these consequences may be, and their extent is hotly disputed, the actuality of a 'left' revival is very different. The left revival has not changed Labour into something other than a parliamentary party. The 'Left' remains dependent on promoting parliamentary representatives and leaders. Those leaders are unlikely to behave as popular fears, media absurdities or the more sanguine constituency activists may believe. Neil Kinnock has shown a commitment to form a broad-based, radical but realistic campaigning position. The post-1983 changes suggest that the parliamentary 'Left' would abandon or trim campaigning shibboleths in the interests of office. The Labour 'Left' is no monolithic entity; it is differentiating under the pressures of national and inner party politics. It is likely that some truce, if not an effective coalition, will be cobbled together. We have not shared the gloom-laden or gloating prognostications of the pundits in the period up to June 1983. However, a real political crisis remains inside the Labour Party. It is a crisis about what to do.[2]

The crisis in the LP has definite objective foundations. The rise of the Alliance is not merely a function of the leftward drift of the Labour Party since the mid-1970s. Likewise, the growing strength of the Left is not merely a function of entryism and conspiracy on the part of forces essentially alien to Labour's spirit, as the hysteria about *Militant* or the Kogans' 'revelations' about the Campaign for Labour Party Democracy (CLPD) suggest. The 1979 defeat precipitated this crisis, and the defeat itself had its immediate foundations in the failure to deal with the problems of the economy. But Labour's crisis about what to do has been developing over a longer term and, for all the importance of Labour's economic policy failures, there are major problems in areas of social policy as well. There are economic constraints on social policy provision which the Left is too ready to discount, but it must also be recognised that there are serious problems with the forms in which services are delivered by both national and local government. At both levels Labour in government has promoted economies of scale and administrative provision in ways which have left many services vulnerable to financial pressures and which have often been highly unsatisfactory to many of their recipients. This has told against Labour's claim to be the party of the welfare state. The LP has been sensitive to the first of these problems – to economic constraints – and too often indifferent to the second.

Neither the programmes of the SDP nor of the Labour 'Left' and the remainder of the party represents an adequate answer to Labour's crisis of policy. Policy has differentiated in response to the conditions faced by the elements of the 'old' Labour Party, but that differentiation has not led to a solution. The SDP's opportunism and its attempts to attract 'anti' voters mean it has less need of such effective answers to promote its own political advance in the short run. Labour, on the other hand, must actually be able to tackle Britain's social and economic problems, and as a condition of its political success it needs to be *seen* to be able to do so. In this respect Neil Kinnock's stress on not concentrating on the content of policies, assuming them to be broadly satisfactory and rather concentrating on putting them over, is misplaced.

The 1979 defeat is commonly ascribed to Healey's 'monetarism' represented by public expenditure cuts and a restrictive incomes policy. Labour fell because of the failure of this policy to tackle unemployment, the perceived burden of taxation on working-class incomes, and the constraint on public sector wage rises which led to the 'winter of discontent'.

Is there a parallel here with the then Labour government's response to the 1929 crash? At that time the Labour Cabinet stuck to 'sound finance', believing that there was no realistic alternative. The result was a split in the party which led to the formation of a National Government composed of Labour defectors and the Tories which carried out 'orthodox' deflationary policies. Labour was shattered by electoral defeat and reduced to a rump. It drifted in a leftward direction and spent the next decade in the political wilderness – a débâcle catalogued in Ben Pimlott's *Labour and the Left in the 1930s*. Does the post-1979 split represent a parallel, with the rise of the SDP, the political negation of the Labour Right and the increasing militancy of the Left? The parallel is far from exact and there are significant respects in which the political and economic conditions of the 1980s differ from those of the 1930s. Labour suffered a crushing defeat again in 1983 and the Tory victory appears to indicate that enough people do believe its claim that there is no alternative to policies of systematic economic depression and the run-down of public services. However, the Tories are unlikely to be able to parallel the success of the National Government confining Labour to the wilderness. But the parallel nevertheless has some merits, for it raises the question of policy alternatives and can help to clarify the nature of the policy crisis faced by Labour.

Is there an alternative to the modern version of economic orthodoxy and sound finance? Many would answer that there is and that Labour failed in 1974–9, largely because it did not implement its 1973 programme and that it lost in 1983 because the leadership did not stand fully behind the new version. This is too facile an answer. Healey's 'monetarism' was no mere function of political timidity and reactionary short-sightedness. It reflects, in a negative, uninventive way, real constraints on policy, many of which the Left's alternatives barely recognise, handled through the administrative and policy instruments available in the Treasury. It is now widely accepted that in the 1930s there was a real alternative, represented by Keynesian policies, and these policies became possibilities once Britain had gone off the Gold Standard.

However, the nature of the constraints on economic policy have shifted since the 1930s and there is certainly no easy 'Keynesian' or other alternative policy of reflation available today? Why? We can answer by looking at the differences between the current depression and that of the 1930s.

Firstly, in the 1930s, Britain had been driven off the Gold Standard and as a consequence interest rates and the exchange rate were separated. It would therefore have been possible to use falling interest rates to expand domestic investment. Since 1945, the UK has been forced by a long-run deficit in the balance of payments to force up interest rates in order to attract foreign holdings of sterling. Further, today the UK currency is more vulnerable than it was in the 1930s to monetary movements on the part of large foreign holders of sterling balances. The central bank cannot control the exchange rate through using its reserves to buy sterling. The UK economy is therefore vulnerable to a balance of payments constraint if it tries to reduce interest rates and promote industrial investment through borrowing without seriously restricting household incomes.

Secondly, in the 1930s both prices and interest rates were falling; this, in combination with excess industrial capacity and some freedom of manoeuvre internationally, made possible an 'inflationary' policy based on government spending and credit creation. We now face a tendency to inflation plus high interest rates – both government finance and credit creation policies are constrained by the inflationary effects of expansion in public spending and by the effect on interest rates of public borrowing and credit creation. Mrs Thatcher's government has staved off inflationary pressures only at the price of systematic government-induced depression. Healey's 'monetarism' was a reluctant reflection of these constraints.

Thatcher's is a willing acceptance of them.

Thirdly, in the 1930s British industry was characterised by 'excess capacity' whereas in the 1980s the phenomenon confronting us is 'de-industrialisation'. Since the early 1970s British firms have shaken out the surplus labour retained to provide capacity for the 'go' periods of the post-war cycle. They have adjusted capacity downwards to meet restricted demand and the effects of foreign penetration in manufactures. British industry faces strong foreign competition in finished manufactured goods and imports many components and machine tools. Any stimulation of domestic demand tends to lead to an 'imports' boom' which strengthens the balance of payments constraints. Further, a rapid increase in demand would in all probability lead to a greater market share for foreign competitors unless the politically difficult step of across-the-board import controls were adopted. In a period of reflation British firms will still be able to sell all they can make, but they will be reluctant to expand capacity or take on extra workers because they will not anticipate a sustained expansion of domestic demand. The relevant experience here is the Barber boom of the early 1970s. This led to rapid import penetration and a rapid choking off of the expansionary policy before British internal expansion had got under way. We have idle workers but all too few factories with unused capacity demanding substantial extra labour inputs in which to employ them. Full employment involves creating new productive facilities rather than bringing workers back into existing ones.

Fourthly, in the 1930s unemployment was largely confined to certain industries and regions; there were also new and growing sectors of the economy such as motor cars, consumer durables and private housing and new expanding regions in the South East and Midlands. Today such 'growth' sectors are more difficult to identify, unemployment is more widespread and there are no regions where vacancies exceed the number of unemployed.

Fifthly, in the 1930s protectionism was a general phenomenon. Britain could therefore have protected home industries by tariffs and hoped to utilise imperial markets. Today we face a depression at the end of a period of massive expansion in foreign trade and the reduction of trade barriers. Advanced industrial countries now trade manufactured goods one with another to a much greater degree and the most successful ones, such as the Federal Republic of

Germany and Japan, are reluctant to lose foreign markets. The UK
has no automatically privileged trade areas like the old Common-
wealth and has suffered a massive decline in its relative importance
as a trading partner outside the EEC. The EEC is now Britain's
main trading partner. The consequence is that the UK economy is
less able to reflate behind a barrier of protective tariffs. Domestic
consumers want foreign manufactures. Domestic producers need
imported components and machine tools. Foreign trading partners
are stronger and less sympathetic to British protectionism. Selected
import controls may well prove necessary, but they should be
negotiated with our EEC partners rather than Britain trying to go it
alone. It is good to see signs that Labour is less dogmatically anti
the EEC.

But Britain's internal economic problems must be solved. The
primary problem now, as in the 1930s, is unemployment. Unemployment is now a major concern of the voters and a fundamental
standard by which the actions of political parties are measured.
Between 1984 and 1990 any government committed to full
employment will need to create some 5 million jobs (allowing for
some 4 million unemployed and a further million joining the labour
force). No reflationary scheme so far proposed promises to create
more than a million and a half jobs. To offer less than full
employment, merely a reflation that gives some limited relief, may
appear the more 'realistic' option. But in the long run it cannot
offer a serious answer to the problems of British society or a secure
future to Britain's youth. Labour must aspire to more than the SDP,
it must offer more than minimal relief from monetarism. If Labour
is to offer more it should not be less than full employment, and to
aim for this as a policy objective rather than a pious hope must
involve a realistic assessment of the task to be undertaken. To reach
full employment over the life of a single parliament would involve
enormous sums in additional public expenditure and credit
creation. A serious attempt at full employment would hit the
constraints outlined above head on. This is not an argument for
simply refusing the attempt, but the policies would have to meet
these constraints in effective ways. Any such policies must involve
radical institutional and social changes if they are to be successful.

Solutions to Britain's current economic crisis have of necessity to
be radical ones. But Labour has no programme adequate to the
task. The re-vamped versions of the 1973 policies, now called the

Alternative Economic Strategy (AES), are alike in proposing economic measures which leave certain crucial aspects of British institutions largely untouched, in particular the position of the trade unions and of free collective bargaining. 'Bennery' both offers too little as a policy of reflation and is stricken by a blinkered conservatism when it comes to the sorts of controls and innovations needed to expand output and employment whilst dealing with inflation and the balance of payments constraints. It places too great a reliance on the capacity of British industry to 'regenerate', to provide new products and production processes in a very short time.

The solution is urgently needed. The period for effective action is all too short for it is in the 1990s that the contribution of British oil production to the balance of payments will begin to tail off. There is no room for failure.

There is no 'answer' to Britain's economic and social problems which does not involve real sacrifices from all classes of the employed population. In a stagnant economy prey to inflation in which there is no prospect of simply using budgetary deficits to mobilise excess capacity to eliminate unemployment, the objective of a full-employment economy which lays the basis for growth and rising living standards must involve the redistribution of existing income and wealth. A large part of this redistribution must necessarily be from the employed to the unemployed, from the wealthy and better-paid to the poor and low-paid. We cannot achieve our objectives by 'soaking the rich', the sums just do not add up. We can only boost public spending on health, education and welfare, on job creation and industrial reconstruction at the expense of higher taxation or higher inflation. Inflation at a rate significantly above present levels is not an easy option, precisely because the UK economy is highly dependent on exports and is already a high-cost, low-profit producer. We cannot eliminate unemployment at the price of poor international competitiveness. To aid the poor and unemployed (who incidentally suffer most from inflation) others must accept a restriction of their standards of living (in the sense of private disposable income – collective consumption should increase) for some considerable time. We are not in the fortunate position of being able to pay for social justice out of growth. This message will be as unpopular with employed manual workers as it will be with the middle classes and wealthy. In the short run it appears a vote-loser. This is the primary objective foundation of the Labour Party's problem – 'realists' may therefore reject a genuine attempt to reduce unemployment in the interests of short-term electoral success. Those 'realists' include the TUC and the Left, for their programmes are defined by the upper limits of political acceptability, in their own perception, not the actual needs of the economy or of the unemployed. But unemployment is greatly feared both by individuals themselves, whether employed or unemployed, and for its wider social consequences. Prolonged mass unemployment and the decline of public services will produce increasing social disorder and personal suffering.

Tory monetarism concentrates losses on the unemployed and the quality of public services to the benefit of the well-to-do and everyone who values private affluence over the costs of public squalor. The question is, can we persuade the mass of the electorate that efficient public services, greater social justice and an attempt to eliminate unemployment are a better alternative, even if this involves higher taxes and discrimination against the well-to-do? Labour has tended to rely on the argument that we can grow our way out of stagflation if we manage the economy right and that we can do so without real sacrifices. Reconstruction is possible but not such a painless reflation.

Several points need to be raised about the conditions of such a 'reconstruction', and we use the word advisedly in the sense leftist parties in Europe did after the Second World War. After several years of Tory rule it will not be possible simply to pick up the reins of government and return to the practices of the 1960s and 1970s. It will not be desirable either; the damage the Tories will have done to existing forms of welfarism and the nationalised sector, whilst in no sense desirable, will offer a chance to re-think and to break with the pattern set in 1945. These points are:

1 Labour should not simply re-nationalise as it did with the steel industry, but re-think the economic role of public sector industries, and above all else their forms of management and public accountability.

2 Likewise the priority cannot be simply to spend more on health, education, welfare and environmental services but to re-think the ways in which such services are delivered and their

administration can be made accessible to influence by their recipients.

3 The structure and finance of local government needs to be thoroughly reformed, to allow both genuine local autonomy and controls to ensure such authorities offer acceptable levels of service. This must involve both the devolution of some central government functions to strategic regional authorities and the decentralisation and democratisation of local 'borough' level services.

4 Restoring competitiveness in key manufacturing sectors, and job creation, are two different tasks. Short-term industrial regeneration will not increase employment in manufacturing. And the long-term prospects of increased employment in the public sector and services depend on the growth of a healthy industrial base. The Tories are not wrong about this. But they are dangerously misguided in their strategy for the private sector. They are maliciously indifferent to the suffering they create.

5 Sustained reflation requires a control over private disposable incomes, and high levels of taxation, in order to finance public investment. There is no scope for painless growth through credit creation and tax concessions. Reflation will mean sacrifices from almost all sections of the employed population. The funds needed for private investment and public spending can only come at the expense of consumption. Reflation cannot be sustained without a radical, redistributive incomes policy. Otherwise a halt would be called by inflation and a balance-of-payments crisis.

The Alliance and sections of the Labour Right accept the need for an incomes policy. But – like the Labour Left – which assumes we can solve our problems while leaving the unions and free collective bargaining untouched – they have no conception of just how radical some policies must be if they are to win sustained assent from workers. A sustained incomes policy is not simply one measure among others: it is a dramatic and irreversible change in political relationships.

6 Incomes policy cannot be a matter of a two- or three-year wage freeze. It must be a complete change in our system of determining incomes and their distribution. Compliance will not be obtained through union bashing. Reform of the unions is certainly needed. But if there is to be compliance in a sustained incomes policy, these reforms must involve greater consultation

at national level, and workplace industrial democracy. The Left would accept both as goodies in a shopping list of policies; but only on the basis of existing, unreformed union structures and bargaining practices. This is simply a conservative and blinkered refusal to face the need for social change.

7 Reflation must be based on an agreement with our partners in the EEC. Only a common strategy on the part of a number of advanced industrial countries can hope to succeed. A series of protectionist national reflationary strategies, even if conducted by radical socialists, can only lead to 'beggar my neighbour policies'. A common EEC strategy offers both some hope of success in the industrial West *and* the prospect of a package which does not ignore the needs of the Third World.

Reconstruction is possible, but not without real sacrifices and major institutional reforms. There are several reasons why it is important to recognise that the necessary changes cannot simply be imposed by government. Some of these concern the conditions of acceptability of government policies. Reconstruction will involve extensive controls, an incomes policy, greater redistribution through taxation and public benefits, selective import controls with inevitable costs to British consumers. These controls and the associated sacrifices and institutional reforms will be acceptable only if several conditions are satisfied.

Firstly, genuine benefits and results must be convincingly promised and they must be delivered.

Secondly, policies must be justified as part of a positive programme of social and economic reforms capable of tackling widely recognised popular concerns relating to the problems of our society: unemployment, inflation, crime, law and justice, humane and civilised provision for the growing proportion of old people in our society, and so on. Socialists may wish to argue for the importance of other issues, not yet generally recognised as matters of social concern. We would want to insist on the importance of many of the issues raised by feminism and the women's movement over the last decade or so. But that is no reason to discount matters of generally recognised current concern. These are issues that cannot be taken up or discarded according to ideological preference. They must be tackled by any social or political force claiming to be able to take a lead in British society. Recognition of the existence of these issues, the identification of constraints on their resolution and the promulgation of effective solutions is a major element in long-term political success.

Thirdly, a radical programme of social and economic reforms must be based on a comprehensible set of general social concerns and principles of social organisation. There is more at issue in this reference to principles than the need to provide a sop to Labour's left-wing activists. The scale of sacrifices, controls and reforms required for a serious programme of social and economic reconstruction means that no merely ad hoc or pragmatic justification would have a hope of receiving the necessary popular support. A major failing of Labour's attempts to present alternatives has been that it offers packages of policies, like the AES, but does not struggle hard enough for the social grounds on which they must be based. Labour can win over public support, but only if it makes a serious effort to change public opinion and to deal with the attitudes and values it embodies. The policies required to deal with Britain's social and economic problems involve radical choices between social alternatives that will not be supported on pragmatic grounds alone. Labour must develop policies which take up its traditional concerns with egalitarianism, democratisation, provision of services on the basis of social and individual needs rather than ability to pay, anti-racism – and to these we would add firstly our concern with the multifarious forms of oppression and discrimination that contribute to the differential positions of women and men in our society, and secondly the generalisation of competencies. This last requires further comment. 'Generalisation of competencies' is an abstract expression intended to convey not simply the need to counter specific discriminations on the basis of race or sex, but also the importance of promoting the widest possible access to certain competencies and skills which constitute crucial means of individual and collective action in modern Britain. It involves a commitment to education in which skills and competencies may be acquired, and the provision of resources so that they can be made available to the largest possible number of people. Generalisation of competencies will involve sacrifices, the diversion of resources to those least favoured in our society, in order for them to acquire relatively complex skills and the means of social participation such that more of the people can take responsibility for political action.

Fourthly, popular support alone will not suffice to ensure the effective implementation of policies. There are key groups whose support, or at least compliance, could prove decisive. We have already referred to the importance of Labour's record as a more or less effective party of government, capable of commanding the respect of leading administrators in the civil service and local government and of management in the major public and private corporations. The alienation of these groups would be a poor foundation for further advance. We have also insisted on the need for an incomes policy and for real sacrifices on the part of large sections of the employed population. Without the active support of shop stewards and union officials there is little prospect of these being accepted in important areas of British industry or in the public sector.

Closely related to this last point is a further reason why the necessary changes cannot be imposed by government, namely that many of these changes depend on initiatives being taken by non-governmental agencies, organisations and individuals. We have insisted that discussion of policies for Labour must not be restricted to policies for *Labour-in-government* precisely because the active involvement of unions and their members is an essential ingredient in any realistic union reforms, and in the revitalisation of British industry and the growth of industrial democracy. Or again, action by and within unions is necessary to combat racism and the many discriminations that affect the relative position of women in employment and the labour market. These points suggest that the social concerns and principles involved in Labour's policies should serve, not merely as slogans but as means whereby ordinary people can think through and organise their involvement in politics. What we have called the generalisation of competencies and the popular acceptance of responsibility will have an important part to play here. A major deficiency in left Labour policy consideration is that it tends to be conducted in statist and commandist terms – yet another instance of Labour's institutional conservatism. The social concerns and principles involved in Labour's policies must relate to the actual concerns of members of the Labour movement, and also to the wider and varied values of British society. These concerns and principles cannot be those of a 'workerist' exclusivism, since Labour has to reach, organise and change other social forces and individuals. At present the LP and the Labour movement organise no more than a substantial minority of the British people.

We have stressed that Labour's programme of policies for social and economic reconstruction should be based on a comprehensible set of social concerns and principles of social organisation. But it is important to be clear about the ways these concerns and principles can operate in the development or assessment of policies.

In considering which principles should guide policy we should bear in mind three criteria for assessing their relevance.

Firstly, *they should assist in resolving problems of social organis- ation*, that is, problems which must be tackled by any social or political force claiming to be able to take a lead in British society, irrespective of its ideology. These problems cannot be chosen or discarded according to ideological preference nor ignored: unem- ployment is one such. The recognition of the existence of such problems, the constraints governing their solution and the promul- gation of effective solutions is the key to long-run political success.

Secondly, *principles must serve as guides to policy and therefore be amenable to providing criteria for assessment of states of affairs.* They cannot be equivalent of an 'other worldly' ethic, in secular terms a millenarian or utopian social programme. Hence the use of principles must be coupled with an opposition to 'schematic thinking' about politics. By 'schematic thinking' we mean the development of a political programme indifferent to the conditions of mass compliance and to the resolution of the actual problems of social organisation. This is not primarily a challenge to the more dogmatic and programmatic elements on the Labour Left. The monetarism of Friedman and Hayek represents the clearest example of such 'schematic thinking'; it is bastardised with bureaucratic opportunism in actual Tory policy. Such right-wing thinking and practice is indifferent to both social and administrative com- plexities and to popular demands and needs. Labour can rightly present itself as a party of principled practicality in contrast.

Thirdly, *principles must serve as a guide to and a pattern for mass conduct*, and not merely as a basis for, or means of, the calculation of political elites. For all the rhetoric of political mobilisation and mass involvement on the left of the Labour Party, the practice of inner-party agitation leads them to ignore the mass of the British people. The people do not merely need to be 'persuaded' or 'educated' that Labour policies are good ones, we need to involve people in thinking about politics for themselves. Labour needs to do much more real grassroots organising, not merely in chosen circles of favoured minorities or the activists of the Labour movement. It must make an effort to reach and involve the white working class and as many of the middle classes as possible. It must enable them to take its politics seriously and that means involving them, getting them to use Labour's political ideas and principles for themselves. This is no easy task, and it cannot be accomplished in a matter of years. A great deal of it will have to take place *after* and not before an electoral victory, in the type of social change Labour initiates. The idea that Labour must make itself a 'mass party' as an *alternative* to seeking electoral victory in the near future is a profoundly short-sighted one. Labour must regard this as a task it must continue and accomplish *in* government, and must change its attitude to its role in government accordingly.

The general social concerns and principles we propose do provide a significant set of conditions for the development of Labour's programme of social and economic reconstruction, but there are other important conditions and constraints, in particular, the various conditions of compliance and acceptability discussed above. For example, an egalitarian position which ignored popular demands for consumption and individual preference would be doomed. In this case a strong educative effort would be required precisely because the post-war boom has strengthened a wide-spread commitment to competitive individualism and the virtues of private benefits. Or again, proposals for democratisation have to relate to generally recognised problems and concerns. Industrial democracy cannot be imposed on an indifferent workforce. If it is to secure support and active involvement it must relate to issues of genuine concern to the workers in question. The same goes for local government. Similar points would apply to democratisation of council housing administration or of the provision of health and other services. Democratisation involves a complex amalgam of parliamentary and representative democracy, popular democracy, local control and self-action. It should not be identified with any one organisational form or mode of representation. To be a viable principle democratisation has to involve acceptance of a variety of mechanisms of effective and efficient decision-making in different spheres of social organisation.

Our final point against any schematic derivation of policies from principles is that specific policies always require decisions involving other principles and considerations. The impact of industrial democracy, for example, would be considerably affected by the way the relevant constituencies are defined and the particular organisational machinery involved – as opponents and defenders of the Bullock Report's proposals clearly recognised. Or again, an egalitarian element in incomes policy and redistribution through taxation and social benefits will require decisions as to whether policies are to operate over individuals or households and those decisions will have differential impacts on the relative positions of women and men, the married and the unmarried.

If there is to be a 'new model party', it must be a party capable of national leadership, uniting its factions in the interest of tackling the problems of the country. An end to internal strife will come only with viable policies that are able to unite Labour's warring factions. Labour failed in 1979 and 1983, because it could not offer a programme which intelligent voters, worried about the state of our society, could turn to with any confidence that it would bear fruit.

Unemployment has ceased to be primarily the concern of the unskilled and low-paid. Even the professional middle classes look to their children's future with fear. The decline in public services threatens all but the very wealthy – even the middle classes who have been the main recipients of post-war welfarism. Increased employment, and the growth of public services, are intimately linked. We have to convince manual workers and middle classes alike that more jobs and decent welfare facilities have to be paid for.

We remain convinced that the electorate will respond to the sincerely expressed prospect of a more egalitarian and fairer society, without dole queues and closed hospitals – but only if they are honestly told what has to be done and the costs of doing it. Labour must start on this task now, or it will be too late.

Notes

1 This chapter has a very chequered history. I wrote an early version of it at Easter 1982 and its basic arguments and judgments remain unaltered. It was intended as the overall introduction to a volume by the editors of *Politics and Power* and others on the policies and principles the Labour Party should adopt at the next election. The volume was overtaken both by the growing political demoralisation of some of the board as Labour's crisis unfolded and by the complexity of the changing features of and debates in the Party. Barry Hindess and I re-wrote the piece but left it in abeyance until after the June election. We subsequently published a shorter version in *New Society* (29 September 1983) just before the Labour Party Conference. The favourable reception of that article led me to revise and publish the larger version. I am grateful to Barry Hindess both for his help in re-writing it and for his generosity in allowing me to publish it in this collection.
2 We wrote an earlier version of these words in the spring of 1982. We thought then that Labour might achieve its post-June reconciliation and a change of leadership in time to stave off electoral disaster. Clearly, Eric Hobsbawm was right in his *Marxism Today* (October 1983) article that too many people in the party did not put beating the Tories first.

Chapter 8

Obstacles in the Parliamentary Road*

Many European Marxists are increasingly aware of the deficiencies of Marxist political theory and of the need to adjust theory and programmes to the conditions of struggle in Western Europe. This has produced a new openness toward the propositions of the 'classics' and a willingness to re-think political lines. This new openness is not the exclusive possession of one party or one theoretical 'school' in modern Marxism but is widely shared among different and diverse political and philosophical orientations, from Carrillo to Poulantzas. It involves the registration of certain basic political conditions as the starting point for theory and policy; these are:

(i) that there are no prospects for an insurrectionary road to power in contemporary Western capitalist countries, and that the working classes of the different countries remain socially and politically fragmented, with substantial portions of manual workers continuing to support non-socialist or even reactionary political parties;

(ii) that, therefore, the classic opposition between revolutionary Marxism and the social democratic 'parliamentary road' can no longer be sustained, the Leninist conception of a vanguard party must in consequence be rejected; instead Marxist and socialist forces must work to build parliamentary majorities around programmes capable of winning mass electoral support, and

*First published in *Euro-Red*, No. 9.

these programmes must necessarily involve political compro-
mises and work through strategies of 'structural reform' (at least
in the initial stages);
(iii) that conventional parliamentary politics are insufficient,
parliamentary representation and struggles need to be coupled
with an active mass movement;
(iv) that this mass movement must involve an alliance between
the traditional socialist forces (parties, trade unions, militants,
etc.) and the new groups engaged in a range of specific struggles
but which can (given the right kind of *socialist* politics) join in a
broad anti-capitalist alliance, notably the ecological and the
feminist movements.

Poulantzas's *State, Power, Socialism* can be placed squarely
within this new attempt to create a democratic and revolutionary
socialism adjusted to the conditions of struggle in the various
Western European countries. In this book he attempts to revise and
adapt his theory of the state to the current conjuncture, re-thinking
and revising previous positions. His new contribution shows that
there is almost as much difference *between* theorists and politicians
who accept this need to re-think Marxism as there was between the
parties, sects and thinkers of traditional 'revolutionary' Marxism.
This difference is inescapable and should not be lamented; there are
strategic dilemmas which cannot be resolved by fiat or the
possession of the 'correct line'. It can also be constructive if the
different strands in this re-orientation of Marxism and revolutionary socialism remain able to communicate with, learn from and ally
with one another.

Poulantzas offers a valuable corrective to the right wing of
'Eurocommunism'. He challenges the, perhaps dominant, current
in European Communist and socialist parties which instead of
adjusting to the conditions of parliamentary struggle capitulate to
the narrowest forms of electoral opportunism and also base their
strategies for socialist transition on an exaggerated legalism and an
over-estimation of the capacity to use existing state apparatuses
and practices to introduce 'alternative' policies. In this respect he
attempts to retain the elements which are valuable in the classic
Marxist thesis that socialism cannot be built simply by utilising the
existing state machine, but without falling into the illusion that it
can be 'smashed'. The state apparatuses cannot be displaced either

rapidly or root and branch under conditions of parliamentary democracy and the maintenance of civil liberties. Likewise Poulantzas accepts that in such a parliamentary-popular strategy the existing organisations of the Left cannot be displaced in favour of a new vanguard party, they represent definite social forces which must be won or neutralised. Thus in criticising the existing Communist and Socialist parties in France he does not attempt to counterpose to them a new model of organisation. In this respect he differs radically from much sectarian criticism of Eurocommunism and left social democracy.

I will not hide that I have numerous differences with the theoretical basis of and his way of formulating these criticisms and proposals. But I consider these to be a secondary issue. In this chapter I will concentrate on what I regard as the positive elements in Poulantzas's contribution. These seem to me to be threefold. Firstly, he presents a clear and valuable critique of the classical opposition between representative and popular democracy. Lenin, following Marx, argued that a direct democracy of soviets was the necessary form of transitional state. Poulantzas correctly recognises that such bodies as soviets cannot on their own check or control, let alone dominate, organised political parties and centralised state apparatuses. Further, we might add that planning and the socialisation of production require such centralised state institutions. Poulantzas asks the following question:

> Was it not this very line (sweeping substitution of rank-and-file democracy for representative democracy) which principally accounted for what happened in Lenin's lifetime in the Soviet Union and which gave rise to the centralising and statist Lenin whose posterity is well enough known? (*State*, p. 252)

It is to Luxemburg that he appeals for the grounds of his criticism. But *both* Lenin and Luxemburg based their conceptions of democracy in revolution on the notion of a spontaneous active working-class mass movement which derived coherence and direction from its class experience and class interests. In this way it could control its leaders and democratically oversee left and state organisations. Lenin relied on the existence of this spontaneous movement to give his notion of soviet democracy credibility, as can be seen from his critique of Kautsky. Kautsky's *Dictatorship of the*

Proletariat offers a more searching challenge to Lenin precisely because he was all too well aware that the modern centralised state cannot be smashed at a blow (indeed socialism would extend its co-ordinating and administrative role), that there is no spontaneous and directed mass movement independent of definite forms of political organisation, that these forms which lead the masses are not subject to their direct control, and that without a *social majority* a revolutionary leadership must use centralist and authoritarian state forms to preserve its power against opposition. Lenin ridiculed Kautsky's distinction between proletarian dictatorship as a 'form of government' (authoritarian statism) and a 'political condition' (a politically organised social majority which neutralises opposition). Lenin was right to castigate Kautsky's legalism and his belief in the capacity of parliaments to control state apparatuses by legislation. He was also right to say that Marx did not make Kautsky's distinction, but that is not a strength – Marx had no developed concept of the party and hence no need to pose the problem of authoritarian *left* centralism. Kautsky's distinction points out that representative democracy is not merely a matter of civil liberties but of the *political function* of those liberties, that they enable political organisations to work out alliances and differences in an open way. Further, representative democracy provides a sign of the social basis of different lines, it measures (however imperfectly) the current social basis of support for different lines. Kautsky is hardly a popular thinker today, the label 'renegade' has stuck, but of all the social democratic critics of Leninism his points remain the most pertinent today. We cannot rely on a spontaneous mass movement-to-be (a movement which objective conditions will make possible) in order to remedy or render valid the forms and lines of left organisation. It is a pity that Poulantzas did not turn and confront this heritage which we have all too easily renounced.

Secondly, Poulantzas realises that if socialist forces must come to power under the political conditions set by parliamentary democracy and begin to construct socialist relations under those conditions then the orthodox notion of the 'dictatorship of the proletariat' must be abandoned. If representative and popular forms of democracy, parliamentary and extra-parliamentary struggles are *combined*, as they must be if an ineffectual statist social democracy is to be avoided, then individual civil liberties and rights of struggle for organisations must not only be retained but enhanced. This will provide opportunities for the right. But this retention of civil liberties is vital *for the left* (it is no mere concession to the bourgeois 'rules of the game'); it makes possible the adjustment of differences, the communication between factions, which can be the only way of preventing a split between maximalist popular and legalist parliamentary wings as occurred in Chile and threatens in Italy. Poulantzas is therefore right to criticise Balibar, however correct the latter may be about the attitude of the classics, for a dogmatism which is 'incapable of advancing research by a single inch'.

Thirdly, Poulantzas recognises that although we may have to reject the political practices associated with the dictatorship of the proletariat that *concept* contains a political lesson which cannot be abandoned: existing state apparatuses, the practices of establishment parties and existing forms of legality cannot simply be utilised and retained wholesale if the objective of the party holding an electoral majority is to begin to construct socialist relations or even to achieve far-reaching reforms. To this extent Balibar is quite right to oppose the opportunist and ultra-legalist tendencies in the Parti Communiste Français. Poulantzas also recognises that the classic theoretical basis for this lesson, the notion of the state as an instrument of the ruling class which must be smashed because it can only serve the bourgeoisie, is completely inadequate. For him state apparatuses and state power are not *homogeneous*, the state is not a unitary entity and is not the exclusive possession of any class. The state is also not a mere instrument of repression or ideological occlusion (as the classics maintained) but a definite organisation with various economic and social effects which cannot be simply displaced. The state has a materiality which cannot be reduced to its class role – state apparatuses are not reducible to state power. State apparatuses and state power can be used in conjunction with popular struggles to transform the state, to limit and displace other apparatuses and powers. But only if a definite strategic analysis of particular nation states is constantly carried out as part of political calculation, analysis which demonstrates the ways in which left forces can act within and against the state. The transformation of the state is a protracted process, not least because its apparatuses are not administrative tools but are relatively independent political sites capable of transformation in their 'allegiances', role and power. Power is not fixed according to the dictates of constitutional law. Unlike opportunism, which merely displaces theory, Poulantzas's approach shows the need for a continuing theorisation *of* the political as a means of political calculation. In respect of his analysis of the internal composition and relation to classes of the state *State, Power, Socialism* advances considerably over his formulations in earlier works (although the result is far from theoretically consistent this is not a bad sign but a reflection of genuine re-thinking).

Poulantzas's work is a commendable attempt to break out of the sterile confrontation between parliamentary opportunism and dogmatic 'revolutionary' Leninism. Fortunately, the attempt to avoid the terms of this opposition is now increasingly widespread, within as much as against the European CPs. But having praised Poulantzas's attempt to re-think the problems and possibilities of a democratic socialism I must also indicate where he fails to go far enough in his challenge to the now almost 'orthodox' Euro-communist parliamentary strategies.

In continuing to treat the state as a 'representative' of class society, dominated by the hegemonic fraction of the ruling class (albeit as a complex 'condensation' of class fractions and forces) and in continuing to argue that the capitalist mode of production in its current phase creates the objective conditions for a certain balance of class interests and class forces (continuing his more extended analysis in *Classes in Contemporary Capitalism*) Poulantzas limits the radical innovations made possible by his treatment of the state as neither homogeneous nor a class instrument. In that earlier work he was concerned to demonstrate the objective conditions for a class alliance led by the working class, a problem he *shares* with many European CP writers on strategy however much he rejects the notions of an 'anti-monopoly alliance' and cautions that the 'new' petty bourgeoisie are as fragmented and politically unstable a class as the old. The original draft of the *British Road* . . . located the basis for a politically organised *social majority* in an objective coincidence of the 'interests' of different classes, fractions and groups against big capital. Poulantzas is too sophisticated to commit himself in this way, he insists on the complexities of the class struggle and of current situations. Nevertheless, in this latest work the *possibility* (although not the certainty) of a democratic transition continues to be located in the objective class situations (and the 'interests' deriving from them) constituted within the current phase of the capitalist mode of production.

The problems with this position for political strategy and political analysis are twofold. Firstly, that class 'interests' are not socially given independent of their 'representation' by political organisations – a point made by Kautsky nearly eighty years ago. Secondly, that there is no social mechanism which brings the working class into organisations which articulate its 'objective' interests as they are identified by socialist theory – a point *not* made by Kautsky who relied on the objective tendencies of the mode of production to create the appropriate conditions of political struggle. Since the Erfurt Programme was written politics in capitalist countries have refused to resolve themselves into *class terms*. I would contend that what democratic strategies must come to terms with is that there is no way in which the political organisations, issues and forces we encounter in contemporary states and political struggles can be said to correspond to the conditions or issues of class mobilisation posited either in classical or in modern Marxism. Leaving aside the theoretical arguments about this (and Barry Hindess and I have argued on numerous occasions *why* this is the case), currently existing political issues have a diversity and a specificity which eludes 'class analysis'. They cannot be avoided for that reason, they are the substance out of which a democratic socialist politics must be made.[1]

Marxists recognise this and yet refuse to come to terms with it. Poulantzas argues, like the *British Road . . .*, that a political alliance must be built out of a complex of issues and forces which are in confrontation with modern capitalism and the modern state. Prominent among these are the feminist and ecological movements.[2] But the problem is that these broadly-based democratic movements cannot be thought of in terms of *class* alliances nor can they be brought in any direct way under the 'hegemony' of socialism. Feminism and ecologism are not articulations of specifically class interests or issues; often the expressed objectives of important organisations or trends within these movements are not compatible with those of traditional socialism nor are they as organisations willing to concede the priority of socialist objectives. Alliance with such organisations and mass movements must be thought of in new terms and not through the place of classes in the contradictions of the mode of production. This is also true of other issues and forces like nationalist and regionalist groups, oppressed minorities, 'special interest' organisations like pensioners, claimants, etc. Socialists have all too often allied with such groups opportunistically, a possibility *reinforced* by the class conception of alliances (all popular forces are objectively on 'our' side!). The *political* alliances constructed through democratic politics by means of which a social majority (in Kautsky's sense – 'hegemony' in the way Eurocommunists tend to use Gramsci) have a complexity, diversity and specificity which will not make *socialist* leadership easy. The organised 'interests' of the popular political forces are by no means always compatible.

Poulantzas is far from having 'parliamentarist' illusions about the capacity of left governments to legislate socialism into existence. But he does not examine sufficiently in this book the effects of the conditions which parliamentary forms can impose on the Left and on mass struggle. To a certain extent this is because he treats contemporary democracies in terms of a 'dominant mass party' which serves as a relay between the powerful centralised executive of the state and the specific organised 'interests' and the masses, a relay in which elections are largely formal and secondary. He cautions of the danger of socialist parties coming to fill this function, as in the Federal Republic of Germany. But in a sense the problems are more basic than this, they concern the possibility of getting genuinely 'left' governments, even minority or compromised ones, elected *at all*. The conditions of contemporary parliamentary democracies by no means favour the left. I cannot make an analysis here but I will offer some pointers.

Firstly, we may begin by noting that contemporary capitalisms continue to create (as they did in Bernstein's time) a mass social base of opposition to socialisation and egalitarianism. This base is extremely diverse in class terms. The distribution of income and wealth, whilst unequal, still endows masses of people (including many manual workers) with the means of a comfortable existence. Further, the policy of governments, including Labour ones in this country, has been to promote ownership of property and saving through the tax system and other incentives. State subsidies and financial capitalism link millions of people to property ownership (housing) and the possession of financial assets (savings, pensions, insurance, etc.). Millions of the people need to be convinced that the nationalisation of land, banks, insurance companies and so on does not materially threaten them. This is even more the case in a country like France where small enterprises remain an important sector in both industry and agriculture. This is less a matter of class interests than of *policy-generated interests*, manual worker owner-occupiers are a case in point. Policy can reinforce the social base of the dominant parties by measures that are genuinely 'popular' and really do improve the material circumstances of masses of people.

Secondly, there is no such thing as 'parliamentary democracy' in general — always specific electoral systems and constitutional arrangements. These are the products of politics and do not deal evenhandedly with the forces that compete in terms of them. This has been notorious since the Social Democrats protested the outrageous electoral laws of Prussia, and it continues today: the blatantly presidential-authoritarian constitution and the voting system in France were deliberately devised to work in favour of the party of established authority and the executive, and has done so all too well.[3]

Thirdly, elections are almost always matters at the political choice of the governing party. Established governments can often set the terms of elections at politically favourable moments. Also state apparatuses are not absent from elections; blatant gerrymandering and open coercion from police, local authorities, etc., are commonplace, as for example under the Karamanlis regime before 1967 in Greece.

Finally, it is not merely a question of *exclusion* from the state machine. The greater the political freedom and competition of organised 'interests', the more open and differentiated the state apparatuses to various political bodies, the greater the capacity either for specific reforms or for blocking unacceptable measures by means of influence and political channels, the greater the potential for the popular and left forces to be fragmented on issues and into competing groups. Much as Poulantzas may deride Dahl's 'polyarchy', to the degree that it exists it offers strong tendencies toward the decomposition of any opposition bloc.

These points may appear 'obvious' but they demonstrate that there is no more certainty about the *first stage* of a democratic road than there is for the success of a revolutionary *coup d'état*. The ultra-Left have drawn the 'obvious' lesson from the coup which ousted Allende; let them savour it, and recognise that the parliamentary Left still has a great deal to learn from the protracted

struggle which was required to put his weak coalition government
into power. The parliamentary 'road' is not an easy one – to be fair
to Poulantzas he is clear about that. But if left governments cannot
easily be elected, it should be realised that practice in respect of the
state apparatuses and established political forces pose a continuing
political problem for left strategy. Abstention from existing
political areas is not possible, there is no political vacuum. This was
the great weakness of pre-1914 German socialism; in such
conditions of exclusion from office the left cannot withdraw from
conventional modes of political influence (however unrewarding)
nor can it neglect extra-parliamentary struggle. Existing non-left
parties and state apparatuses articulate interests, serve as representatives for forces, promote or block measures of policy or reform.
Trade unions, interest groups, minority parties/factions must
continue to deal with the established parties and apparatuses. How
to win measures which extend the capacities of popular movements, how to avoid manipulation and division through the
strategies of powerful opponents are strategic problems to which
much more thought needs to be devoted because they are likely to
be with us for a long time. The problem with 'adjusting' to the
conditions of parliamentary democratic struggle in the West today
is that they are conditions in which the Left and popular forces are
more often than not likely to be divided and far from the formal
seats of power.

Notes

1 For a fuller account of these theoretical arguments see Cutler *et
al.*, *Marx's Capital and Capitalism Today*, Vol. 1, Part Three and
for an extended critique of Poulantzas's positions on class in
Classes in Contemporary Capitalism see Paul Hirst, 'Economic
Classes and Politics' in A. Hunt (ed.), *Class and Class Structure*.
2 To these movements would now have to be added the European
peace movements. Anti-nuclear politics and socialist politics are not
necessarily allied, as the Mitterrand government's commitment to
modernising France's nuclear deterrent shows.
3 Since this was written the Left has indeed formed a government
in France, but the protracted struggle needed to do so confirms the
anti-Left bias of the electoral system.

References

Althusser, Louis, 'Ideology and "Ideological State Apparatuses"' in *Lenin and Philosophy and other Essays*, London: New Left Books, 1971.

Althusser, Louis and Balibar, Etienne, *Reading Capital*, London: New Left Books, 1970.

Anderson, Perry, 'The Origins of the Present Crisis', *New Left Review* 23, Jan./Feb. 1964.

Anderson, Perry, 'The Myths of Edward Thompson – Socialism and Pseudo-Empiricism', *New Left Review* 35, Jan./Feb. 1966.

Anderson, Perry, 'Problems of Socialist Strategy' in P. Anderson and R. Blackburn (eds), *Towards Socialism*, London: Fontana, 1965.

Anderson, Perry, 'The Components of the National Culture', *New Left Review* 50, July/August 1968.

Anderson, Perry, *Passages from Antiquity to Feudalism*, London: New Left Books, 1975.

Anderson, Perry, *Lineages of the Absolutist State*, London: New Left Books, 1975.

Anderson, Perry, *Considerations on Western Marxism*, London: New Left Books, 1976.

Anderson, Perry, *Arguments within English Marxism*, London: New Left Books, 1980.

Balibar, Etienne, 'Self-Criticism', *Theoretical Practice* 7/8, Jan. 1973.

Bhaskar, Roy, *A Realist Theory of Science*, Hassocks: Harvester, 1978.

Braudel, Fernand, *The Mediterranean and the Mediterranean World in the Age of Philip II*, Vol. I, London: Collins, 1972.

Callinicos, Alex, *Is there a Future for Marxism?*, London: Macmillan, 1982.

Carr, E. H., *What is History?*, Harmondsworth: Penguin, 1964.

Chayanov, A. V., *The Theory of Peasant Economy*, Homewood, Ill.: Richard D. Irwin, 1966.

Cohen, G. A., *Karl Marx's Theory of History: A Defence*, Oxford: Oxford University Press, 1978.

Collingwood, R. G., *The Idea of History*, Oxford: Oxford University Press, 1961.

Collingwood, R. G., *Autobiography*, Oxford: Oxford University Press, 1978.

Cutler, A. J., 'Letter to Etienne Balibar', *Theoretical Practice* 7/8, Jan. 1973.

Cutler, A. J., Hindess, B., Hirst, P., and Hussain, A., *Marx's Capital and Capitalism Today*, Vol. I, London: Routledge & Kegan Paul, 1977; Vol. II, London: Routledge & Kegan Paul, 1978.

Elvin, Mark, *The Pattern of the Chinese Past*, London: Eyre Methuen, 1973.

Feyerabend, Paul, *Against Method*, London: New Left Books 1975.

Foucault, Michel, *The Archaeology of Knowledge*, London: Tavistock, 1972.

Foucault, Michel, *Discipline and Punish*, London: Allen Lane, 1977.

Freud, Sigmund, *Civilisation and its Discontents* (1930) in *Standard Edition*, Vol. XXI, London: Hogarth Press, 1961.

Gane, Michael, 'Althusser in English', *Theoretical Practice* 1, Jan. 1971.

Gane, Michael, 'Lenin and the Concept of Conjuncture', *Theoretical Practice 5*, Spring 1972.

Ginzburg, Carlo, *The Cheese and the Worms*, London: Routledge & Kegan Paul, 1980.

Hacking, Ian, 'Language, Truth and Reason' in M. Hollis and S. Lukes (eds), *Rationality and Relativism*, Oxford: Basil Blackwell, 1982.

Harris, Lawrence, 'The Science of the Economy', *Economy and Society*, Vol. 7, No. 3, August 1978.

Hegel, G. W. F., *The Philosophy of History*, New York: Dover, 1956.

Hegel, G. W. F., *Lectures on the History of Philosophy*, Vols I–III, London: Routledge & Kegan Paul, 1955.

Hindess, Barry (ed.), *Sociological Theories of the Economy*, London: Macmillan, 1977.

Hindess, Barry and Hirst, Paul, *Pre-Capitalist Modes of Production*, London: Routledge & Kegan Paul, 1975.

Hindess, Barry and Hirst, Paul, *Mode of Production and Social Formation*, London: Macmillan, 1977.

Hindess, Barry and Hirst, Paul, 'Labour's Crisis', *New Society*, 29 Sept. 1983.

Hirst, Paul, *Social Evolution and Sociological Categories*, London: Allen & Unwin, 1976.

Hirst, Paul, 'Economic Classes and Politics' in A. Hunt (ed.), *Class and Class Structure*, London: Lawrence & Wishart, 1977.

References

Hirst, Paul and Woolley, Penny, *Social Relations and Human Attri*, London: Tavistock, 1982.
Hobsbawm, E. J., 'Labour's Lost Millions', *Marxism Today*, Octc ..., 1983.
Kautsky, Karl, *The Dictatorship of the Proletariat*, Ann Arbor, Mich.: University of Michigan Press, 1964.
Kogan, David and Kogan, Maurice, *The Battle for the Labour Party*, London: Fontana, 1982.
Lacan, Jacques, *Ecrits*, London: Tavistock, 1977.
Lakatos, Imre, *Philosophical Papers, Vol. I – The Methodology of Scientific Research Programmes*, Cambridge: Cambridge University Press, 1978.
Levine, Andrew and Olin Wright, Erik, 'Rationality and Class Struggle', *New Left Review* 123.
Lukács, Georg, *History and Class Consciousness*, London: Merlin Books, 1971.
Marcuse, Herbert, *One Dimensional Man*, London: Routledge & Kegan Paul, 1964.
Marx, Karl, *Capital*, Vol. I, Moscow: Progress Publishers, 1965; Vol. II, Moscow: Foreign Language Publishing House, 1961; Vol. III, Moscow: Foreign Language Publishing House, 1962.
Marx, Karl, *The Eighteenth Brumaire of Louis Napoleon Bonaparte* (1852) in Marx, Karl and Engels, Frederick, selected works, Vol. I, Moscow: Progress Publishers, 1968.
Marx, Karl, '1857 Introduction' and '1859 Preface' to *A Contribution to the Critique of Political Economy*, London: Lawrence & Wishart, 1971.
Marx, Karl, *Grundrisse*, Harmondsworth: Penguin, 1973.
Midelfort, H. C. Erik, 'Madness and Civilisation in Early Modern Europe: A Reappraisal of Michel Foucault' in B. C. Malament (ed.), *After the Reformation*, Pennsylvania: University of Pennsylvania Press, 1980.
Pimlott, Ben, *Labour and the Left in the 1930s*, Cambridge: Cambridge University Press, 1977.
Poulantzas, Nicos, 'Marxist Political Theory in Great Britain', *New Left Review* 43, May/June 1967.
Poulantzas, Nicos, *Classes in Contemporary Capitalism*, London: New Left Books, 1975.
Poulantzas, Nicos, *State, Power, Socialism*, London: New Left Books, 1978.
Rowbotham, S., Segal, L., and Wainwright, H., *Beyond the Fragments*, London: Merlin, 1979.
Sahlins, Marshall, 'The Original Affluent Society', *Stone Age Economics*, London: Tavistock, 1974.
Sartre, Jean-Paul, *The Problem of Method*, London: Methuen, 1963.

Sassoon, Donald, 'The Silences of *New Left Review*', *Politics and Power* 3,
    London: Routledge & Kegan Paul, 1981.
Sen, Amartya, *Poverty and Famines: an Essay on Entitlement and
    Deprivation*, Oxford: Clarendon Press, 1981.
Shaw, W. H., *Marx's Theory of History*, London: Hutchinson, 1978.
Thompson, Edward P., *The Making of the English Working Class*,
    London: Gollancz, 1963.
Thompson, Edward P., *The Poverty of Theory*, London: Merlin, 1978.
Winch, Peter, *The Idea of a Social Science*, London: Routledge & Kegan
    Paul, 1963.